# IN SPITE
# OF EVERYTHING

# DR. ROBERT A.
# RUSSELL

Audio Enlightenment Press

*Giving Voice to the Wisdom of the Ages*

Printed in the United States of America


First Printing, 2022
ISBN 978-1-941489-85-7


www.RobertARussell.Org

# Table of Contents

Introduction ................................................................. v

Chapter I.   In Spite Of . . .

Bottlenecks ...............................................................1

Chapter II.   In Spite Of . . .

Difficult People.........................................................15

Chapter III.   In Spite Of . . .

Resentment.............................................................27

Chapter IV.   In Spite Of . . .

Disease ...................................................................41

Chapter V.   In Spite Of . . .

Human Opinion ......................................................53

Chapter VI.   In Spite Of . . .

Handicaps...............................................................71

Chapter VII.   In Spite Of . . .

Marital Difficulties .................................................91

Chapter VIII.   In Spite Of . . .

The Threat of Divorce .............................................111

Chapter IX.    In Spite Of . . .

The Responsibilities of Parenthood........................................123

Chapter X.    In Spite Of . . .

The Fact That They Will Grow Up .......................................137

# Introduction

Why are you reading this book? We have to assume that the title interested or challenged you. We have to assume that from experience you know what it is to meet with a difficulty that must be overcome, to climb a mountain that seemingly has no crest, to follow a trail that has proved endless, to endure a pain or sorrow from which there seems to be no escape.

These are experiences common to man. Unfortunately, the will to overcome "in spite of everything" is less common. Fortunate is the individual who learns that obstacles, heights, and barriers do not have to be conquered by the will alone, who learns that since he is one with God, he has access to all the Might and Power and Majesty of the spiritual kingdom.

This book is for the man in search of knowledge of his spiritual power and of the way to use it wisely. This book, then, is for everyone. Deep in man's heart is his desire to live a good life, to earn promised blessings, to help build a better world. Universal experiences tend to reinforce the knowledge that all men are brothers and that the spiritual man triumphs in the end.

Someone has wisely said that there are in the end only two motives for action. We act "in spite of" something or "because of" it. In reality the two are one, for determination to overcome, to conquer, to demonstrate power depends upon the ability to sense the need and the awareness of potential power to meet it. The end result is the same whether we act in spite of opposition or because of encouragement.

May you find the help you seek as you study these pages!

*Robert A. Russell*

# Chapter I.    In Spite Of . . .
## Bottlenecks

"What is this wall of Jericho that faces me?" asks a man who is meeting with repeated failures. "What is this unfriendly power that moves against me and destroys my efforts?"

"Why can't I put this deal over? Why does it hang fire? Why don't these people come to terms? Why don't they make up their minds?" inquires another baffled business man.

A housewife laments, "Another month gone and we've just met expenses. Can't we ever get ahead the way other's do?"

The use of the word *bottleneck* to describe a condition that checks progress is a happy choice for those who enjoy figurative speech. We know immediately when we hear the world that there is a congestion of some sort — that power of some kind is attempting to move through a channel that is too small for it. We have bottlenecks in traffic, on the sales floor, in the business office, and in transportation areas. But the serious bottlenecks are those that occur in our spiritual lives.

The important thing in a bottleneck in which you are involved is not what is happening or not happening in the material world, but what is happening to you as you experience it. What is the trend of your mind? What do you intend to do about the delay or defeat? What are you going to make of it?

Are you big enough to see it as a challenge? To accept it as a warning? To be grateful for its occurrence?

There are persons who have grown so accustomed to misfortune, to repeated set-backs to chronic ill-health that they apparently accept their state and live with it without much rebellion. They don't know a bottleneck when they see one.

The Truth student, however having experienced the harmonious living that results from the realization of man's unity with God and having accepted the attributes of God as his, should be instantly alerted when the pattern of his living changes.

He should be quick to recognize a bottleneck and to ask, "Why should I fail to solve a problem of this kind when I have overcome so many like it, when I have helped others to overcome similar problems? What is the matter with me? Why do my prayers and treatments fall upon stony ground?"

In turn I ask of him, "How long have you been studying Truth? How many demonstrations have you had? You still believe in the Omnipotence of God despite this delay? You still believe in the power of God to make man free?"

"Certainly I do," is his response.

The barrier to actions, the bottleneck to progress, the hurdle in the race must then be found. Since the Law is perfect and the good we seek is already in manifestation, the conclusion must be that the source of the trouble is within the seeker.

There are many possibilities for causes of temporary failure. Let us think through them one by one.

## Case 1. The Over-Complacent

What do the Scriptures say? *"Let him that thinketh he standeth take heed lest he fall."* It is very easy after one has made many demonstrations in prayer to fall back into slipshod ways of materialistic thinking and living. It is easy to forget that continued success in prayer requires daily discipline of the mind. The soul grows through exercise just as the muscles do. It fails from lack of use; it grows on resistance.

It is strange, isn't it? You are in need of something, and God offers it to you. But you are unable to take it. Why? Because you are not in the proper mental state to receive it. Somewhere along the line you have gotten off the track. You have gotten separated from your Source.

Perhaps this sounds confusing and intricate, but it isn't. Then water come to a barrier in the stream, it does not stop or give up. It goes around the barrier. It changes its course. So it is with the stream of consciousness. Your bottleneck means that you are going in the wrong direction. It is God's way of telling you that you must change your course.

If this case has a personal interest for you, think through the paragraph that follows. Does any suggestion help you to see the area in which you are at fault?

Maybe you have been trying to demonstrate by your won ability. Perhaps you have not let God do His part. Have you been resting in the letter of the Law, forgetting the power of the Spirit? Did you not realize that familiarity with the letter might tend to breed contempt? You may have to put your problem in God's hands and then reach out for it again. You may have forgotten that God is unchanging Law and tried to get Him to go your way instead of going His. Did you pray for healing and continue to think and talk sickness? Did you pray for prosperity but fear and talk poverty? Success in treatment requires positive thinking when the cupboard is full as well as when it is empty.

## CASE 2. THE NOW-OR-NEVERER

An understanding of time as a factor is important to one who is seeking the solution to a problem.

The searcher should look squarely at the impasse in which he finds himself and realize that in a month or in a year, it will be such ancient history that *"the place thereof shall know it no more."* He should understand that its only power comes now from the attention he is giving it—attention that rightfully belong to God. He should try to remind himself of the problem that engaged his attention a month ago, or perhaps even a week ago. The chances are that he can't recall it clearly. Then the action indicated certainly is to lay this problem aside for a time.

Our advice to him is this: "Stop working so hard. Let God take over. Change your course. Instead of trying to get God to go your way, go His way. Time is not important. Try to grasp the fact that there is no time but NOW. What you desire has spiritual existence. Your recognition of this fact gives it power to manifest itself in your life. The NOW of its appearance depends upon the clarity of your vision, the persistency of your thought, and the degree of your acceptance."

## Case 3. The Giver-upper

Do you remember what Eliphaz said to Job?

> *"You have yourself set many rights,*
> *and put strength into feeble souls;*
> *your words have kept men on their feet,*
> *the weak-kneed you have nerved.*
> *But now that your own turn has come, you droop;*
> *it touches you close, and you collapse."\**

Answer me, you who have given up. Do those words bite your soul?

Many Truth students are like Demas. They make a good start but a poor finish. St. Paul in his letter to Philemon speaks of Demas as a trustworthy and promising disciple. In his second letter to Timothy, he says, *"Demas forsook me."* What a familiar ring this report has! Here today and gone tomorrow! One day up and the next day down! One day strong and the next day weak!

The story of Demas is the story of a man who made a wonderful beginning but a bad ending. Demas — my friend, my partner; Demas — my fellow worker. *"Demas forsook me."*

Demas gave up before he had reached his goal. Demas couldn't hold on. He had no staying power. Have you ever met Demas? Then look into your mirror. Yes, my friend, there is a Demas in every man. He is that something in each of us which tends to crumble under pressure.

---

\* Moffatt Translation of the Bible.

Paul is given a prominent place in the Bible, but Demas is mentioned only three times. "But Paul was a failure," you say. That is true. Paul failed in many things, but he himself did not become a failure.

Paul had a quality of consciousness and faith that enabled him to see life through to the end. His approach to difficult problems was like that of the stone mason splitting a block of granite. Every blow makes its mark, but the last blow splits the block. So it is in spiritual work. Efficiency comes out of persistency. The dauntless man will not only repel disaster but bring victory out of defeat.

Demas is a symbol of the divided mind. His loyalty was divided between God and the world. There was no staying power in his religion. He followed Christ but had never been captured by him. His Christianity was like a tent easily put up and easily taken down. He had faith but not enough of it to carry him through. He was suffering from halfwayness.

When a man exhibits skill in handling difficult situations, it is not that he has more favor with God than other men but that he knows better how to face his problems. He has a finer quality of consciousness and a firmer grip on Truth.

In fair weather, Truth students look pretty much alike. In storms, their defects come to light. Trouble gets some persons down, but it lifts others up. The attitude of the successful person is the attitude of Job: *"Though He slay me, yet will I trust Him."* If our reaction to trouble is affirmative, trouble will make us better, strong, and nobler. If it is negative, it will make us bitter, weak, and ignoble.

Many people fail in a crisis because they do not have a faith equal to their needs. Like Demas, they grasp the outer aspects of the Christian Gospel but never get beyond the symbols. They have words, words, words, and nothing to support them.

If you are a Giver-Upper, you need to be honest with yourself. Are you putting first things first? Do you constantly practice the Presence of God, or do you just call upon Him when you are in trouble? Do you discipline your thoughts and emotions? Do you have regular periods of silence, meditation, and spiritual reading?

## CASE 4. THE HALF-AND-HALFER

There is a sign on a radiator in certain hotel that says, "Please turn the radiators all the on or all the way off. If they are turned only partially on, they will leak and be noisy." Is the implication clear? Are you a partial Christian? Then you must turn the radiator all the way on.

Perhaps that is what is wrong with your prayers and treatments. Your demand is half-hearted. It does not reach the great Creative Power; it touches only the margin of your possibilities.

No matter how impossible, how incurable how improbable a situation or condition may seem to you, God's power to act in it is limited only by the degree of your acceptance.

The saying, "Man's extremity is God's opportunity," is true only if we surrender the problem in it's entirely into His hands. What is there about this "do-or-die" attitude in a crisis that brings about an instant manifestation of God's power and deliverance? Isn't it the sudden awareness of our own inadequacy to cope with the problem? Isn't it the realization that Jesus had when He said, *"I can of my own self do nothing"?*

These words did not emanate from despair or defeat but from an understanding that God is the One and only Source of all help. Man's extremity is God's opportunity because there is no time in a crisis to work out the problem for ourselves. We are compelled by the very nature of the need to let go of the problem and to accept Divine Guidance and help. *"Then shall thy light break forth as the morning and thy healing shall spring forth speedily: and thy righteousness shall go before thee: the glory of Jehovah shall be thy reward. Then shalt thou call, and Jehovah will answer: thou shall cry, and he will say, Here I am."*

## Case 5. The Windmill Tilter

Perhaps the cause of your trouble is hidden deep in your subconscious mind. It may be an old negative belief or fear that you have not yet uprooted. It may be the effect of a childhood experience that you have forgotten. Trying to fight this cause unscientifically is just as effective as tilting at a windmill.

Jesus said of the subconscious mind: They *"are like tombs whitewashed; they look comely on the outside, but inside they are full of dead men's bones and all manner of impurity."** Buried deep in the subconscious are race beliefs, doubts, fears, inhibitions, and complexes. A slight movement in experience may bring an unexpected evil into manifestation.

---

* Moffatt Translation.

A violent antipathy toward an individual or situation, and an unreasoning anger, an unfounded rejection may appear with such suddenness that you are completely baffled. If you can analyze your difficulty or ascertain its cause, you are well under way to free yourself from it. If you do not know the source, you must declare your freedom from every form of evil and your complete dependence upon God.

The subconscious mind itself is the avenue by which we reach God most directly and through which He acts. Declaring freedom from every form of evil so persistently and with such confidence that the Truth becomes a part of one's consciousness cause the subconscious to create conditions for living that are free from evil. There is no problem, wall, or impasse that can resist the power of the subconscious.

In metaphysics, we say that the Truth manifest itself by means of It's Consciousness in you. There is a condition to be fulfilled. If the conscious mind goes in one direction and the subconscious in another, there is an impasse or bottleneck. To get good results in prayer both phases of mind must go in the same direction — that is, the acceptance must be complete. *"Whosoever . . . shall not doubt in his heart* [subconscious mind], *but shall believe that what he saith* [in the conscious mind] *cometh to pass; he shall have it."* Treatments that are not consistent with Principle can never reveal the power and perfection of God.

History has been made by those who have accepted the challenge of difficult situation and triumphed over them "in spite of everything."

Bottleneck experiences follow many patterns. For Jacob, it was a wrestling match. For David, it was the death of his son. For Socrates, it was the cup of hemlock. For St. Paul, it was a shipwreck. For John Bunyan, it was a prison. For Washington, it was Valley Forge. For Lincoln, it was a gun in the hand of a madman. For Sir Walter Scott, it was crippled limbs. For Disraeli, it was racial prejudice. For Steinmetz, it was rheumatic pains. For Franklin Roosevelt, it was polio.

"In spite of everything!" Was a powerful phrase that is! It implies not only an unconquerable spirit but a resolute will. It produces an attitude that brings man and God together in an unbeatable combination. If a man has that attitude, he can meet any difficulty and overcome it. If he does not have it, he is ineffective, and his work is unavailing.

# WHAT TO DO IN BREAKING A BOTTLENECK

## 1. THANK GOD FOR IT.

A bottleneck is a signal. If it were not for the stone wall that stopped you, you might have gone on to your destruction. To thank God for it is not only to make your agreement with your adversary but to arrest his power. The bottleneck says, "You are getting nowhere; it is time to change your course."

## 2. RELAX YOUR GRIP.

If God is going to work the problem out in Divine Order, He must have perfect freedom. Psychologist tell us that there is no problem that the subconscious mind cannot solve if the individual will just become still enough to let it do its work. How does one secure this stillness? We have the answer in the 112th Psalm: *"He shall not be afraid of evil tidings; his heart is fixed, trusting in the Lord."* The way to get the mighty power of God flowing through the subconscious mind is to keep the thought centered on Him.

### 3. BE CONFIDENT.

Cultivate faith and trust. Say many times a day: "I can make this demonstration because the Power in me can." Put feeling and imagination into your declaration. Know that the power of God is flowing through every thought and word.

### 4. BRING GOD INTO THE SITUATION.

Identify yourself with His Power. A wall is what the name implies—a solidification of belief. You do not storm or dynamite the wall; you shake it down by taking your attention away from its appearance and by centering your thought in God. Like Joshua of old, you cause the wall to fall by blowing upon the trumpet of Truth.

When Paul and Silas were in prison, they took their attention away from the chains and fetters that bound them and centered it in the Presence of God. They began to sing and give thanks for their deliverance, and *"About midnight . . . there was a great earthquake . . . and immediately all the doors were opened."*

Here then is the pattern in dealing with a bottleneck:

Practice the Presence of God, knowing that He is in charge.

Praise Him and give thanks that the bottleneck is being broken.

Affirm with deep conviction —

I KNOW NOTHING BUT THE PRESENCE AND
POWER OF GOD THE IMPERFECT IS GIVING
WAY TO THE PERFECT. THE BOTTLENECK IS
BROKEN. PERFECT MOVEMENT IS RESTORED.

## 5. SEND YOUR WORD FORTH INTO ACTION.

The greatest stumbling block in spiritual work is a sense of
inadequacy. We still carry in our make-up some of the sense
of guilt resulting from the old doctrine of original sin. We
hesitate to accept the Power that is ours, the Place that has
been given us, the Joy that comes with understanding.

When we realize that the Universal Mind flows through us
if a channel is made to receive It, we relieve ourselves of any
sense of guilt and accept gladly the responsibility for creating
the channel.

Say with deep conviction and feeling:

DIVINE LOVE GOES BEFORE ME AND PREPARES
MY WAY. DIVINE LOVE BREAKS DOWN
EVERY BARRIER, ADJUST EVERY IMPERFECT
CONDITION, SMOOTHS OUT EVERY DIFFICULTY,
HEALS EVERY DISEASE, DISSOLVES EVERY FEAR
AND DOUBT, AND CONQUERS ALL WEAKNESS.
MY WORD DISSOLVES EVERY THOUGHT OR
IMPULSE THAT WOULD CIRCUMVENT OR
NULLIFY MY GOOD. THERE IS NOW NOTHING IN
ME THAT CAN DELAY, DEFEAT, OR OBSTRUCT
DIVINE POWER.

## 6. Exercise Courage.

Courage is a state of mind that pushes defeat, disappointment, frustration, and futility aside to make room for victory and success. Courage is the tenacity to hold on when everything goes wrong. It is the faith to persevere when everything seems lost. It is the patience that never tires. It is trust that endures when hope has fled. It is continued prayer when there is no apparent answer. It is determination that does not yield to defeat.

The courageous man does not build up bottleneck and obstacles in his imagination. He depreciates and minimizes them. Repeat these words of Joshua to yourself many times a day: *"Be strong and of good courage; be not afraid neither be thou dismayed: for the Lord thy God is with thee withersoever thou goest."* Repeat them now. Say, too, *"If God be for us, who can be against us?"* Look your bottleneck straight in the eye while you say, "You are a lie. Your life is spent. You have served your purpose. You have no more power to delay my good. I accept only the best. My good is here and now.

## 7. Cultivate Positive Thoughts.

If you think defeat, you will be defeated. If you think delay, you will be delayed. If you think negative thoughts, you will create negative consciousness in which only negative things can take shape. On the other hand, if you think positive thoughts — thoughts of power, thoughts of success, thoughts of enthusiasm, and thoughts of victory, you will create a consciousness in which only good things can happen. Think affirmatively, hopefully, and positively for one day at a time. Feed your mind with such thoughts as these:

TODAY I THINK POSITIVELY ABOUT EVERY PERSON, PLACE, CIRCUMSTANCE, AND THING. IN SPITE OF ALL APPEARANCES, I SEE ONLY THE GOOD.

TODAY I AM FILLED WITH THE EXPECTANCY OF GOOD. I RECOGNIZE ONLY ONE TIME – THE NOW – AND ONE PLACE – THE HERE.

I KNOW THAT MY WORD PENETRATES AND DISPELS EVERY INHARMONIOUS CONDITION AND DISSOLVES EVERY OBSTACLE THAT STAND IN MY WAY. MY WAYS, *"ARE WAYS OF PLEASANTNESS"* AND ALL MY *"PATHS ARE PEACE."* MY CONFIDENCE IS UNLIMITED, FOR I KNOW THAT THE MANIFESTATION OF GOOD IS INSTANT AND COMPLETE.

I NOW IDENTIFY MYSELF WITH SUCCESS IN MY EVERY THOUGHT, WORD, AND DEED. I REPUDIATE ALL BOTTLENECKS AND DELAYS. I CAST OUT EVERY DOUBT AND FEAR; I EXERCISE THE DOMINION THAT GOD HAS GIVEN ME.

### 8. ACCEPT YOUR DEMONSTRATION.

Meditate at least three times a day using the statements outlined or others of your won creating. Meditation specializes the Law and directs its power to the object you have in mind. Thank God for the fulfillment of your desire. Believe that you have it. Act as if the request were already granted. Persevere in your work – *"nothing doubting"* – until your word returns to you bearing the fulfillment of your desires.

# Chapter II.    In Spite Of . . .
## Difficult People

"I wish I could change my boss's disposition. He is getting unbearable. I could cheerfully wring his neck.

"How do you suppose we can keep Jennie from talking so much? She is just like a parrot. It is beginning to get on my nerves."

"How can I change my wife? She is a good woman, but she keeps the neighbors in an uproar."

"How can I change my chief clerk? He is so negative and unresponsive that people are complaining about him."

As one moves among his acquaintances and friend today, he is impressed by the fact that so many persons are out of harmony with themselves and with others. Everywhere one finds some one who is willing to change almost anything or anybody in the world but himself. No matter where we are or where we go, we run into diseased egos. In the church, in the home, the lodge, and in the office, difficult people are among the most pressing of problems. It is human nature to try to meet the difficulty by attempting to make the obnoxious individual over. "How can I change him?" "How can I changer her?" "What can I do to change them?" we ask ourselves.

The truth of the matter is that we cannot change anything or anybody but ourselves. That may come as a shock to the person (the Mr. Fix-It) who is always so busy about changing others, but it is true. Jesus said, *"Let your light so shine before men that they may see your good works, and glorify your Father which is in heaven."* What does it mean to "Let your light so shine"? It means to se the kind of example that will inspire others to change themselves. That is the first part of the process; the other part is to work upon your own consciousness.

You thought this was going to be a lesson about the other fellow, but it is really one about you. Now mark this well. If you did not have an affinity for the disagreeable traits and personality defects that you see in other people, you could not experience them within yourself. You could not see them. It is a fact that what you see to criticise in the other fellow must first be in yourself. Is that a bitter pill to swallow? Let us see why it is true.

You and I live in two worlds at the same time — a world of matter (material things) and a world of consciousness. Between the two worlds there are five senses that keep the consciousness informed as to what is going on in the material realm. Right now you maybe sitting in the mezzanine of a beautiful hotel. You are surrounded by luxurious appointments, furniture, writing desks, pictures and by well-dressed people. How do you know where you are? Your five senses tell you. They relay sounds, sights, odors, and other sense perceptions to the brain, and you then identify yourself with your environment. You tell yourself that you are in the mezzanine of the Waldorf-Astoria Hotel, that an orchestra is playing, and that many people are moving about. In other words, you interpret these impressions in terms of your understanding and your past experience, and you may arrive with a sense of worry, annoyance, and discomfort. Another person in this same environment might get an entirely different response as a result of his interpretation of what his sense report.

It is obvious that people, circumstances, and events are to you what your consciousness reports them to be. That is why Jesus could see good in everything and in everybody. Being filled with the consciousness of God's presence, He responded only to the good. Does this sound too abstract? Then let us put it this way: You do not see a person as he is; you see only your reaction toward him. If the response reports a defect in another, you have a defective consciousness. That is why Jesus said, *"Why beholdest thou the mole that is in thy brother's eye, but considerest not the beam that is in thine own eye?"*

The person who annoys and anger you is not your home or office, but in your own consciousness. You are never dealing with a person. You are dealing only with your own mental reaction to him. Are you finding fault with someone who is malicious, unpleasant, hateful, or annoying? Then you are dramatizing a specific state of consciousness. You are judging another; and by your false appraisal of him, you are judging yourself. You are, so to speak, blaming another person for the fault that is within you. The psychologist would say that you were projecting your own limitations. The unholy habit of criticising others is often only an excuse for not facing one's own weakness. When a man asked Dwight L. Moody how he could overcome his habit of exaggeration, he said, "Why don't you begin by facing the fact that what you call exaggeration in yourself you call lying in other people?" Mood was right. All reformation and reconstruction begin within the self. To transform another person, we must first transform our own ego. When you get right with yourself, everybody else will be right with you. Isn't that a wonderful thought?

How then shall we start this process of change? The fist thing is to weed out from our own consciousness all the negative attitudes that have taken root and to cultivate only positive attitudes. This will require time and effort, but it can be done. If we will check our own motives, guard our thought, and be as indulgent and considerate of other people as we are of ourselves, we can bring about any desirable change.

The second step is to discipline our egos. Each of us must ask himself these questions:

> How do I react with criticism?
>> Do I fly to my own defense? Do I study it to see if it is justified?
> How do I react to my own mistakes?
>> Do I freely admit them? Do I try to cover them up? Do I syndicate them?

Deflating the ego is a difficult task that pays great dividends. After bragging about himself to his boy said, "Yes, son, I am a self-made man."

The son replied., "Gee, dad, that's what I like about you; you take the blame for everything."

Robert Burns said in immortal words.

> "Oh, wad some Pow'r the
>> giftie gi'e us
> To see oursels as ithers
>> see us!"

Some of our friends would be very happy to tell us how they see us, but they know that our ego could not take it. We, as a rule, do not want to be changed. The strongest motivation for change is good example.

The most successful sermon is one that reveals people to themselves, but there is always someone present who expresses a wish that some relative or friend could have heard it. We do not want people to tell us the truth about ourselves; we want them to tell us what we want to hear. When Jesus said of a certain man, *"But he desiring to justify himself"*, he was also talking about you and me. The ego out of control has an instantaneous defense reaction; it always seeks a way out. Right or wrong, we tend to defend or justify what we say or do. We say, "I did it because — — — — —" or "I said it in spite of — — — — — — — —." Perhaps we should pray the prayer of the publican more often, *"God, be merciful to me a sinner."*

It is a salutary thing to deflate the ego periodically. Nowhere is it more important than in one's relations to other people. If you know why you do certain things, that is half the battle. Go over your motives, responses, and reactions and you will be amazed at how you are letting yourself down — that is, how poorly what you do measures up to what you know is good to do. If you catch yourself projecting your own limitations into another, take your ego in in hand at once. Put it in its place. Do you like to assert your superiority? Do you like to talk down to people? Do you like to direct them, regiment them, or change them? Do you demand love and respect? Are you long on condemnation and short on approbation? Do you make it hard for others to discharge their obligations to you? Do you forgive but not forget? Do you high-pressure customers into buying your goods? Do you try to tell to impose your will upon the Divine Will? Do you like to cram knowledge down the mental throats of your children? If your answer is yes to these questions, your ego is diseased. The successful leader in any field is not the reformer but the revelator. The successful salesman does not force his merchandise upon the customer. He creates a desire for it. The successful teacher stimulates thinking by drawing knowledge from within the pupil.

Sometimes I feel like saying to the egotistical, self-important, and self-righteous what Jesus said when he came into Galilee — *"Repent ye, and believe the gospel."* That is — Shift the load. Get right with God. Get on the right side of the law. *"Let your light so shine."* Don't get all puffed up. Don't brag. Don't push. Don't shout. We know you think you're on top of the heap. Come down off your perch and be one with us. Fill your mind with the consciousness and the presence of God, and nothing but good will come into your life. If you want to change other people, you have only to change yourself. You have only to heal yourself of what you think is wrong with them.

*"Let your light so shine before men that they may see your good works and glorify your Father which is in heaven."* Can you glorify God without receiving something yourself? Can you let our light shine without lifting your mental level? Would you change the other fellow? Then be an example to him. Show him what is means to live up to the best that is in him. Make your example so attractive that it will create in him a desire to change himself. This is not only the most painless and effective way to change others, but he only way. *"By their fruits,"* said Jesus. *"ye shall know them."*

St. Paul said *"Be ye transformed by the renewing of your mind."* When you realize that you are the only thinker in your world, you will see that the only things that have to be changed are your states of mind, your reactions, and your responses.

Disagreeable people are not "out there" but "in here" — here in your consciousness. They are to you what you conceive them to be. They react to you according to your mental image of them.

A person is not essentially ugly, cantankerous and difficult, regardless of his appearance. He needs to meet just one person who is big enough to see what he really is in order to make that reality visible to everyone. Since you and the offender are both in the One Mind, it is in mind that the change must take place.

You do not have to put up with difficult people. Instead, you have to think right about them. Instead of looking upon them with hopelessness, despair, and defeat, see through the appearance of imperfection and behold them as they are in God. Instead of becoming embittered about other people, handle your thought about them. Rise up in the consciousness of Christ Mastery and declare the Truth. Say with St. Paul. *"Christ in you the hope of glory."* Every time you think of an individual whom you have looked upon as a problem say, "I know the Christ is there within you; I shall not rest until He comes forth." Continue treating in this manner until your thought is clear, your attitude true, and all criticism and judgment will have been made. The clarification of your own image of the person who annoys you will have produced the change.

# THERAPY

1. *"Be kindly affectioned one to another."* It would be wonderful if everybody liked everybody else, but there are personal equations in each of us that make this desirable state impossible. The best discourse on personal development is to be found in the Epistle of Paul the Apostle to the Romans, Chapter 12. St. Paul tells us that among many things which we should construe as *"reasonable service"* is to *"live peaceably with all men."* That is good advise, for it takes the depression and anxiety from the dead spots in human relations.

2. Take an interest in unattractive people and love them. This is not easy in some cases, but we shall never find their lovable qualities until we call them forth. If we keep looking for a person's faults instead of his possibilities, he will never change. Jesus always looked for the good in people, and He brought it forth. "In the company of sinners," said Hugh Black, the author of *The Comrade in White*, "He dreamed of saints." If you want to change people, do not try to get them interested in you, but you be interested in them. Give them a chance to talk to you about themselves and their operations.

3. *"A city that is set on a hill cannot be hid. Neither do men light a candle and put it under a bushel, but on a candlestick and it giveth light unto all that are in the house."* Some people are like the stained glass windows in an unlighted church. They appear to be dead inside. But the light is turned on, they glow with warmth and color. They radiate beauty and brilliance. But how does one turn on the light in the soul? By centering his thought in God.

4. Study people with a view to helping them, but study yourself more. If people are always getting on your nerves and upsetting you, it is reasonable to suspect that there is something wrong with you. Maybe your own vibrations are irritating or depressing, perhaps you rub people the wrong way. There is a reciprocal action between inharmonious persons; it is wise to find out which one is projecting the friction. You can determine this responsibility only by analyzing yourself.

5. Practice praise instead of criticism; pronounce approbation instead of condemnation. I f you spend your time criticizing and magnifying the faults of others, you shut out the good. I like the story of Jacob and his sons who went down into Egypt

to buy food. Everything was packed—the best fruits in the land, balm, spices, myrrh, nuts, almonds, and money. Then Jacob said, *"Take a little honey."* Why honey? Because honey would sweeten the journey. It is smooth, kind, soothing; it has all the qualities necessary to win people and make friends. That is what we need in human relations today—honey instead of vinegar, praise instead of censure. When you start out to change people, don't forget to take a little honey. Kindness and praise will turn the trick when everything else fails.

6. If you have a hard time changing your mental concepts of an irascible and unlovely person, try listing his good qualities on a piece of paper. Since Christ indwells every man, you will find spiritual qualities in him if you hunt of them. Make an exhaustive study of him. Try to add something new and good to your list every day. This practice will not only help to glorify the person in your own mind, but it will change your reaction to him. I f you build a new and positive belief about a person into your mind, he will consciously or unconsciously strive to live up to the new belief.

7. Always keep in mind that it is you who must change and not the other fellow. If you get along with yourself, others will get along with you. When your ego is out of control, everybody you meet will probably be a bit disturbing to you. Jesus said, *"By this all men know that ye are my disciples, if you love one another."*

## MEDITATION

SINCE I AM THE ONLY THINKER IN MY UNIVERSEICANCHANGE_____ONLY BY CHANGING MY OWN CONSCIOUSNESS OR MENTAL CONCEPT OF HIM. I REFUSE TO

LET MY REACTIONS OR BELIEFS ABOUT HIM DISTURB MY HAPPINESS OR PEACE OF MIND ANY LONGER. I LOVE GOD WITH ALL MY HEART, SOUL, AND STRENGTH, AND I LOVE _____ AS MYSELF. I SEE ONLY THE CHRIST IN HIM; I REFUSE TO SEE ANYTHING ELSE. I WILL NOT THINK THAT THIS PERSON IN ANNOYING OR DIFFICULT. I REJECT WHAT MY SENSE TELL ME ABOUT HIM. THIS PERSON IS A SPIRITUAL BEING MADE IN THE IMAGE AND LIKENESS OF GOD. I SEE HIM AS GOD SEES HIM—PERFECT, TRUE, KIND, GRACIOUS, AND COOPERATIVE.

I AM HIS FRIEND, AND MY FRIENDSHIP DISSOLVES ALL DISCORD, INHARMONY, AND ILL WILL. MY RELATIONS WITH HIM ARE PERMEATED THROUGH WITH THE UTMOST WARMTH, LOVE, PEACE, JOY, HAPPINESS, GOOD WILL.

## TREATMENT

THIS APPEARANCE OF IMPERFECTION IS NOT TRUE OF GOD; THEREFORE, IT IS NOT TRUE OF _____. I KNOW NOTHING BUT PRESENCE AND POWER OF GOD IN HIM. I CONSCIOUSLY EMBODY ONLY THOSE IDEAS THAT SET FORTH HIS WHOLENESS AND PERFECTION. I REFUSE TO ACCEPT OR BELIEVE ANYTHING ELSE.

Repeat the treatment each time you think of the individual until the old factors of causation are no longer active in your consciousness. You can quicken the process by meeting each old thought as it appears.

Gradually the person will change and your original reactions will wither and die. You will have changed the disagreeable person by changing yourself. You will have broken the bottleneck.

Robert A. Russell

# Chapter III.　In Spite Of . . .

## Resentment

"I gave that clerk a piece of my mind," reports a dissatisfied customer with apparent satisfaction. "He burns me up!" says the clerk about the boss whose demands she considers unreasonable. "Then I blew up!" admits the boss as he tells his his wife about the day at the store and describes the final and climaxing bottleneck.

"I'm so mad at Bill I can't see," says twelve-year old Jim.

"I could murder him," many of us have said thoughtlessly when irritated beyond measure with one individual.

The surprising things about all these careless statements is that they are true.

We say, "I'll give her a piece of my mind," and that is exactly what we do. We give to a disgruntled person something so rare and precious that it cannot be purchased with money.

When we say of someone else, "He burns me up", that, too, is psychologically correct. Anger takes poison into the blood and burns up the cells. It sets the body on fire. It carries destruction to everything within its reach, for anger is a form of insanity.

The words, "I blew up," describe an emotional state that sends a death impulse to every nerve, tissue, and muscle in the body. The speaker wanted to blast the other fellow, but it took him thirty-six hours to get rid of the poison generated in his own body by his one blow-up. He was like the sadistic farmer that Stanley Jones tells about who "tied a stick of dynamite to a hawk, lighted a fuse, then turned it loose, expecting it to blow itself up in midair. Instead, the hawk flew to his barn, and the explosion wrecked the barn."

Jim, too, was telling the truth. Blinded by anger, how could he see? How could he have vision of any sort—physical, mental, emotional?

Murder springs out of murderous thought. If there were no murderous thoughts, there would be no murder. Literally speaking, the one who says, "I could murder him," really wants at the time to murdering some of the finer things within himself. But one of the risks that the sorehead runs is that he may actually harm another.

Louis Gay Balsam* presents some startling and pertinent facts. He says:

"I have interviewed more than 600 persons involved in major traffic accidents. They ranged from laborers and clerks to professional persons and millionaires. I met them at home, on the job, in courtrooms, jails, clinics, hospitals.

"With just eleven doubtful cases—less than two per cent—these people had two frightening things in common: All were deeply unhappy before the accident. And all remembered this unhappiness coming to a head, or an explosion, a few hours before the smashup.

"What has 'blowing one's top' or seriously upset feelings got to do with automobile smashups? That's what I combed jails, courtrooms and hospitals to find out."

---

* Balsam, Louis Gay, :Soreheads at the Wheel Are Deathheads." *The Kiwanis Magazine,* March, 1952.

A row with a foreman (The speaker was "burned up."), a quarrel between husband and wife. (The wife became "blind mad."), gambling losses, and disappointment in love are recognized by the individuals involved as the basic cause of fatal or near fatal automobile accidents. Balsam concludes that "the overwhelming percentage of accidents come to people who have met bitter disappointment, usually that very day. Auto accidents and bruised egos go together. It is as simple and as terrible as that."

What could any of the individuals reporting to Balsam have done in spite of the circumstances? What can the Truth student do when the human factor takes over in the personal equation?

He knows definitely that a change must come to him, to his emotional attitude, to his state of mind. What is there so big, so powerful, so effective that it will produce a change?

*"None of these things move me,"* said St. Paul, and so does the person who has committed himself to the search of Truth. *"Vengeance is mine; I will repay."* A sense of detachment from the immediate source of worry and resentment accompanies the deliberate effort to realize that the age-old truths are true today—that they are personal—that they await only individual recognition and realization to become the motivating, activating, triumphant power, or force, or factor, if you will, in the life of the awakened seeker.

Jesus said, *"Ye have heard it said by them of old time, Thou shalt not kill; and whosoever shall kill shall be in danger of the judgment: But I say unto you, That whosoever is angry with his brother without a cause shall be in danger of the judgment."*

Do you see that anger and resentment always do more harm to us than to the objects of our hatred? It is the law of the boomerang. It is the truth in the old saying, "Chickens come home to roost," and "Like attracts like."

The body is made for serenity and not tension. The mind is made for peace and not confusion. Life is made for love and not hate. The resentful person sells himself down the river. Anger disrupts everything in his life. Hate throws everything out of balance. It affects adversely every organ, nerve, and tissue in the body. The resentful person destroys himself just as surely as if day by day he drank small doses of arsenic. Anger is slow suicide. If you hate, you will be hated. What you send out will return. If you dislike people, they will dislike you. Wrath is a two-way poison. If express it, it will burn you up. If you repress it, it will blow you down.

Closely allied to resentment is malice. If love is the most wonderful thing in the world, malice which grows out of resentment, is the most terrible. Malice is anger and resentment in concentration. It is vengeance and wrath ready to strike. It is the venomous desire to do harm. It is the deadly cobra in ambush. Crystallized malignity and wrath, that is malice.

Resentment is truly an emotional bottleneck. Progress stops, motions ceases, actions is impaired when resentment becomes the motivating force.

Said a member of my congregation, "I have done everything about my stiff leg. I have prayed, but it does not heal."

"Have you resentments?" I asked her.

"Yes," she replied, "I hate the doctor who made the mistake in setting my broken hip."

"Do not pray any more," I said, "until you get rid of your resentment."

She finally made the surrender and was healed. If you want to know what Jesus would do in a situation of this kind, listen to His words—

*"So, if you remember, even when offering your gift at the altar, that your brother has any grievance against you, leave your gift at the very altar and go away; first be reconciled to your brother, then come back and offer your gift."*\*

Why is prayer unavailing under indignation or rage? Because these emotions not only shut out your brother but shut out God. *"Leave your gift at the very altar and go away."* That is pretty strong language; it means to stop all prayer and church-going until you have squared things with your brother.

Resentment not only delays healing but produces disease. It produces disease because it is made of our very life substance. Anger heats our blood, wrecks our health, destroys our peace, shatters our nerves, and nettles our sleep. We hold resentment against friends, neighbors, relatives, business associates, employers, and parents and the end result is conflict, inner decay, neurosis, mucouscolitis, varicose veins, blurred vision, digestive troubles, split personality, and ulcers. Silly, isn't it? Being resentful is just like playing the game of life with loaded dice. Instead of winner over the object of our resentments, we cheat only ourselves.

In an orderly, harmonious, and well-tuned mind, there is no place for animosity, antagonism, bitterness, condemnation, grudges, grievances, or resentments.

---

\* Moffat Translation of the Bible.

5

Robert A. Russell55

"But," you say "I cannot be a human door mat. I just can't let people walk over me. If I don't retaliate, people will think that I am weak." Will they? Did you ever see a camomile plant? The more people walk on it, the faster it grows. So it is with the soul. The more you return good for evil, the faster the soul grows. You become what you return. You keep what you give, whether it be good or ill.

Consider what happens on the plane of human resistance. A man assails you, and personality says that must defend yourself. How do you go about this? You organize an attack by using invectives of hatred, criticism, unkindness, and sarcasm. The eye-for-an-eye philosophy says that you muse use physical force or stinging, hate-filled words in repaying wrath with wrath. Oh no, personality never stops to count ten or to consider whether there is a more effective way to meet mental violence; it just lets go with all the vitriol it can muster. The ego has been attacked and it demand satisfaction. The adversary becomes more and more violent, returning blow for blow.

Like a ball thrown against a wall, hate returns with the force with which it is sent.

Resentment always follows this pattern—

1. The victim feels he has been wronged in some way.

2. He is impelled to strike back before it is too late. He feels he must seek vengeance while there is still time.

3. He meets mental or physical violence by allowing the baser animal instincts to rule. Fear, price, uncertainty, insecurity goad him on.

3255

4. He feels that his resentment is a necessity — that he lets himself down unless he asserts himself in response to what he sees in the situation.

5. The law of the boomerang works. *"With what measures ye mete, it shall be measured to you again."*

There is, too, a pattern for meeting resentment, for diminishing it to the point its disappearance, for sublimating it, for turning it to good, for opening the bottleneck it has created.

# STEPS IN BREAKING THE BOTTLENECK OF RESENTMENT

## 1. REALIZE THAT NO ONE CAN HURT YOU BUT YOURSELF.

*"Be still and know that I am God* [Peace, Power, Love, Truth, Wisdom, Understanding, Knowledge, Justice, Joy, Plenty]." Know that harm comes to you from your adverse reaction to a situation — from your failure to recognize your spiritual brother in the person who offends and not from what is happening or from what any individual does.

Resentment is a problem of the ego. If a man's ego is under control, he is impervious to resentment; you can call him anything you will, but you don't really disturb him. Accuse the average man of being a cheat or a liar, and he will tell you vigorously that you have got him all wrong. But speak the words cheat and liar to the egotistical man, and he will tell you that he hates you. When the ego gets in front of Christ, it screams.

Do not allow disgruntled people to determine your attitude and reactions. If the other fellow has a chip on his shoulder, *"What is that to thee? Follow thou me."* You are to conquer Laotse said, as does "a stream when it reaches a rock; it goes around it, and when strong enough, overflows it."

Just remember that the gossip, the cheat, the slanderer, the liar, and the scandal-monger are what they are because of the evil influences and unfavorable circumstances that have played upon their lives. Mental violence is the only weapon they know. You can rise above them seeing them as God made them. Until they discover the power of Love, they cannot be anything else. To *"love your enemies,"* as Jesus commanded, means to dissolve the hateful, bitter, critical, antagonistic thoughts within your consciousness.

We do not overcome our enemies by saying that we have none but by changing the states of mind that created the enemies. We do not deal with enemies *per se;* we work with the embodiment of our confused ideas. It is not the person we hate that disturbs our health and peace of mind, but the mental act of hating.

When your opponent seems to have the upper hand, disarm him by refusing to function on his level. He is probably not ready for your new attitude and may have to be given time to learn. Your conduct will convince him that there is a power greater than hate and that it can be used by man.

When Jesus met resentful people, he turned the other cheek. That is, He turned away from the disagreeable and hateful in the person and beheld him as he was in God. You can do the same thing.

You may kid yourself into thinking that hatred is justifiable, but while you are deluding yourself you are destroying yourself, too. The reasons for your resentment may seem very real; but if it were not for your self-centeredness, you could not even entertain the thought of resentment. When you are God-centered, there is nothing fore resentment to act with.

## 2. FORGIVE YOUR ENEMIES.

Consider each person from whom you feel the slightest resentment, and forgive him for everything. It doesn't make any difference what an adversary may have said or done, you should heed St. Paul's words, *"Ye should rather forgive him and comfort him."* Why is forgiveness so necessary to the maintenance of mental and physical health? Because it keeps one in spiritual balance. To forgive everybody for everything at all times is to keep ourselves free. When we forgive another, we are doing much more for ourselves than we are for him. Say:

I DO NOT ENTERTAIN RESENTMENT TOWARD ANY MAN BECAUSE IN SO DOING I AM RECOGNIZING RESENTMENT WITHIN MYSELF; AND IN GOD CONSCIOUSNESS, THERE IS NO RESENTMENT. THE LOVE OF GOD IN ME BEARS WITNESS TO THE LOVE OF GOD IN EVERY MAN.

When Abraham Lincoln was taken to task for forgiving an enemy, he said. "Our business is to get rid of this one by turning him into a friend through forgiveness."

*"How many times shall I forgive my enemies?"* asked Peter. *"Until seven times?"*

Jesus replied, *"Until seventy times seven."*

In other words, keep forgiving until resentment dies.

When Jesus gave the command, *"Do good to them that hate you,"* He made it clear that we have a spiritual responsibility for our antagonists as well as for ourselves. No matter how vicious, slanderous, or unkind an enemy may have been, Jesus says that you must do something good for him. Well, what? Shall we throw our arms around him and go tripping down the street? No. That is not what Jesus meant. To eliminate an enemy, He pointed out that we must change our consciousness. Instead of seeing him as he appears, we must see him as he is—a unified spiritual being. The question is not "How can I get even with this bird?" but "What can I do to save him from himself.?"

*"A man's foes shall be they of his own household,"* said Jesus.

Does that ring a bell within you? What about the foes in your mind? What about all the people that you think have harmed you—friends that have disappointed you, relatives that have failed you, confidants that have betrayed you, partner that have cheated you, competitors that have undersold you, rivals that have double-crossed you, enemies that have lied about you, bosses that have lorded it over you, associates that have disappointed you, and superiors that have interfered with your progress? How have you been handling them? Don't bother to make reply. I can see the answer in the lines of your face, the carriage of your body, and the dark circles under your eyes. They shriek, "Poison! Poison! Poison—self administered."

Hate feeds upon hate. It takes two to make a quarrel. What happens when the hated prays for the hater? The hate falls apart, and harmony is restored. The one force that cannot be resisted is spiritual.

*"A man's foes shall be they of his own household."* Early in the ministry, I resented a certain man strenuously. It was an active hatred that never left me night or day. He became my one great obsession. He was with me twenty-four hours a day even though he lived two hundred miles away. This mas was bound to me as if he were handcuffed to my wrist. "Where," I asked myself. "is this evil power coming from? Why can't I shake this personality and get it out of my life forever?" Then came the answer. "You are bound to this man by a cord of your own thinking. *'Loose him and let him go.'*" I discovered that I was holding this man to me by my own hatred.

### 3. Accept the Promise, "Vengeance Is Mine; I Will Repay."

Acceptance of this truth relieves us of the necessity of resentment. We do not have to get even with an enemy; God has already taken care of him for us. The judgment is made even before the antagonist comes out to get us. Yes, even the debtor who takes refuge in the Statute of Limitations is covered. *"Not one jot or tittle shall be removed until the law is fulfilled."*

He who takes anything by subterfuge or cunning, whether it be the peace and happiness of another, his money, or his goods, will in time pay the uttermost farthing. This law is relentless and untiring. It never fails. Human adroitness and cunning try to evade but never succeed. It doesn't make any difference whether you get a bus ride without paying or refuse to fulfill a pledge of money to the support of the work of your church or any other good cause, you will sometime, somewhere lose that much and usually more. It may be taken from you through some other unexpected demand, but the law is exact and impersonal.

Jesus said, *"Resist not evil."* Spiritual resistance is more than non-resistance. It is resistance on a higher level. The non-resistant person does nothing about his adversary except to rise above him. that is, he harmonizes with higher powers that no enemy can effectively resist. When one person in a quarrel ceases to be actively resistant to the other, the quarrel is dissolved. Fire cannot burn without fuel.

Would you resist God who is the only Presence and Power in the Universe? Then why resist one of the children? Hate, like all negative emotions, is a mask *(persona)* of personality. Now forget your pride and look through the mask of the true being of your antagonist. Can you fight what you see there — the inner reality? No! Why not? Because the inner reality is Christ.

*"Vengeance is mine; I will repay."* When we recognize this law and use it, we can solve all controversies by laborless activity. We can bless those who curse us and do evil against us. *"Stand still and see the salvation of the Lord."* This is the pattern by which we live without loss.

**4.** *"RENDER UNTO GOD THE THINGS THAT ARE GOD'S."*

Nothing has to be done on the impulse. The measurement of time is a man-made device. *"For a thousand years are in the thy sight but as yesterday when it is past and as a watch in the night."*

*"But beloved, be not ignorant of this one thing that one day is with the Lord as 'a thousand years, and a thousand years as one day.'"*

Stop ascribing power to persons, places, circumstances, or things. If God is the only power, why do you recognize hate as a power by resisting it? Don't you realize that evil in any form has no power except that which you give to it? Then why exaggerate and strengthen evil by trying to destroy it? When will you learn that "Power belongeth unto God"? Resistance destroys and and scatters power, but love generates it. Would you keep your mental machinery well lubricated? Would you keep friction at a minimum? Then use the oil of love generously.

Spiritual resistance is not following the line of least resistance. It is making yourself a good conductor of power and seeing the Truth of people and circumstances despite their appearance. It is a recognition of the Spiritual Law by which you may live in peace, plenty, and happiness despite the evidence of bottlenecks of many and various kinds and of assorted sizes.

Robert A. Russell

# Chapter IV.  In Spite Of . . .
# Disease

Do you remember the question in the minds of the three women that first Easter morning when they hurried to the tomb— *"Who shall roll us away the stone from the door of the sepulchre?"* The stone was the bottleneck that seemed unbreakable. There was a sense of urgency about their trip, for there was a job to be done. The body of Jesus must be annointed with sweet-smelling oils and spices despite the obstacles in the way—the huge stone, the Roman seal, the Roman guard. Such barriers would have kept most people home. But in spite of all the impediments to action, these three women started out. *"Who shall roll us away the stone?"* (Who shall remove this impossible barrier? Who shall clear the way that we may get into the tomb and do our work?) But wonder of wonders, the obstacle was removed before they arrived at the tomb! The impossible had happened.

Of course, there are difficulties in your way, too, in breaking through the bottleneck of disease of any kind but like these three, you must choose between acceptance of the bottleneck and exercise of faith. If you believe that the stumbling blocks are too much for you and sit down in despair, the bottleneck will remain. But the interesting thing about the Law is that, if you only make a start, It reacts instantly and creatively to your faith. The promise is *"Before ye call, I will answer."* Just walking *toward* your difficulty, and God will clear the road beyond your wildest expectations. The *dynamis* (potentiality) of God within you will become the dynamite of your word. If you will face your difficulty instead of going around it, you will find that your stumbling-block will become a stepping-stone. Like Jacob's ladder, your obstacles will become *"steps into heaven."*

It would be interesting at this juncture to learn just what it is that is troubling you. What is the bottleneck, obstruction, or impasse that you have failed to remove? But it is not important, for it makes no difference what the obstruction is. The Law can and will dissolve it.

The Law does not say: "Behold I heal a headache, but not a cancer." The Law does not know big or little, curable or incurable, malignant or benign.

Perhaps you still believe in the necessity of sickness and suffering, or you may still entertain doubt or uncertainty as to the effectiveness of your prayer. Perhaps it is your unconscious conviction that is at fault. How then can the healing principle operate? Can you see that doubt or uncertainty in giving a treatment becomes a part of the treatment? The Law is exact, immutable, and inexorable. If you still believe that some problems are hard and others easy, you cancel completely the operation of Divine Power. What you need at such a time is absolute confidence in yourself and in your word. If your intention is for healing, you must expect to be made whole in spite of all adverse and contradictory appearances. It is not your body, however, that awaits healing; it is your belief. Prepare yourself for the acceptance of healing by saying many times a day:

THERE IS NOTHING IN MY CONSCIOUSNESS THAT CAN OBSTRUCT THE OPERATION OF MY WORD.

THIS BOTTLENECK HAS NO PLACE IN ME. I REFUSE TO RECOGNIZE IT OR GIVE IT POWER.

I KNOW THAT MY WORD IS POWERFUL ENOUGH TO PENETRATE AND DISPEL EVERY INHARMONIOUS CONDITION. I KNOW THAT MY WORD INSTANTLY REVERSES AND DISSOLVES ANY AND ALL ADVERSE THOUGHTS AND BELIEFS. I AM FILLED WITH FAITH, WITH POWER WITH THE EXPECTANCY OF FULFILLMENT, WITH THE ABSOLUTE CONVICTION THAT SPIRIT IS ALWAYS VICTORIOUS.

THE CHRIST MIND WITHIN ME ENTERTAINS AND EXPRESSES ONLY THAT WHICH IS POSITIVE, LIFE-GIVING, AND PERFECT.

The first thing every sick person should do is to examine his mind as the possible source of his trouble. If the instruments of science have failed to heal the disease, it is almost certain that the seat of the trouble is in the mind, or consciousness. Disease is what the word implies—a lack of ease. It is a state of mind that acts adversely on one's physical and emotional selves. It is an absence of harmony and balance, and this lack opens the body to destructive and foreign elements.

His state of mind is the premise from which one's though and action spring. You act as you think. Your state of mind is your consciousness. You express it in all that you say and do. To change any condition in your life, you must first change your consciousness.

"How do I go about this?" you ask. The first thing to do is to analyze your mind—attitudes, beliefs, feelings, mental reflexes, biases, thoughts and viewpoints, for the outward or overt you is determined by what you are like inside. If there is disease or sickness in the body, there must first be disease and sickness in the soul. For every effect, there is a cause and that cause is always within.

Mind, soul, and body are one. What affects one affects the other.

If you accept this, you will see why it is that the sick man must remove and faulty and negative thought patterns and habits that limit the expression of his soul before he regains health.

If the materialist insists that there is no healing except through medicine, you must remind him of the faith that medicine generates. Without faith in the doctor and his medicine, the prescription would do very little good. The doctor's assuring, encouraging, and uplifting words are factors in many instances more effective and potent than the medicine itself. Jesus said, "*According to your faith be it unto you.*" If your faith is sufficiently strong, you need no outside help. It alone will heal you.

It makes no difference what form of healing you choose, the underlying factor is Faith. If there is anything in your subconscious mind that doubts, divides, or questions the capacity of the Healing Power within you or if your faith is partial or half-hearted, the healing Principle will not operated. "*The Lord your God is a jealous God.*" He is jealous in the sense that He demands your whole mind, strength, heart, and soul. To be spiritually healed of any condition or disease, you must believe whole-heartedly that there is no limit to the God Power to heal, other than the limit of your ability to conceive that Power as healing. The Principle is never limited. Your soul can bring out a condition as perfect as your mind can conceive. The doctor refers to this healing principle as "*Vis medicatrix naturae.*" The metaphysician refers to it as God.

To know God as All-Power and All-Health is essential in spiritual healing. You must recognize and feel the reality of the All-Power. You must believe in It and live It.

Now to get back to the bottlenecks in the mind. Ask yourself these searching questions:

1. What is my attitude toward my environment? Toward people? My family? My friends and my associates?

2. Are my reactions positive or negative? True or false? Normal or abnormal? Wholesome or unwholesome? (Am I unkind? Am I parsimonious? Am I moody and easily discouraged? Am I miserly or niggardly? Am I avaricious? Do I give away to irritation, criticism, and petulance?)

3. Does life with all its ups and downs seem good or bad? Does it inspire me or depress me? Do I think of myself as a cog in a wheel or as the whole wheel?

4. Do I think of myself as being at the mercy of others, a victim of circumstances? Do people get in my way and prevent me from accomplishing my purposes?

5. Have I allowed disappointments and frustrations to harden my heart? Have I interrupted the Life Force by fear, worry, anxiety, anger, hate, or jealousy?

6. Am I starving the cells of my body through apathy? Am I dying because of indifference? What has happened to my zeal? How can I hope to stay alive without it?

Just as apathy is a major cause of death, lack of enthusiasm is a major cause of disease. The cynic is on his way out. He is living from the bottom of his life instead of from the top. Failure, frustration, and futility stem from cynicism, and cynicism starts with a loss of faith in one's self. The word *cynicism* comes from the same root as the word *canine*, meaning currish or dog-like. "A cynic is a man with a dog-consciousness, and he lives in a dog's world," someone has said.

Contrast the cynic with the enthusiast. The cynic is pessimistic, distrustful, and gloomy; the enthusiast is optimistic, ardent, and zestful. The word *enthusiast* comes from two Greek word *en-theos* meaning *in God*. The enthusiastic man is a zestful man — alive in every part of his being. The cynic sees life only in the present. The enthusiast sees it as a whole.

Do you begin to realize what unpleasant dispositions, abnormal attitudes, and intemperate thoughts do to the flesh? A bad disposition is just as much a disease as chicken pox. We talk much today about preventive medicine. But most disease is preventable through discipline and moderation of the mind and emotions.

Disease is an outward and physical sign of an inward and psychic deterioration. Reread the preceding sentence and underscore it. If you will think of the body as was moulded by the actions and impulses of the mind and soul, you will see why it is that your sins always find you out.

The body is a barometer of the soul. Whatever happens to the soul happens to the body. If the soul is withered by cramped and wizened thoughts and attitudes, the body will manifest shrinkage. The body is so inextricably woven together with the soul that every breath, nerve, organ, bone, sinew, drop of blood and saliva bear witness to the impulses and reactions of the mind. A negative condition in the soul has a depressing effect upon the whole body.

Do you rail against pain? Then change your consciousness. Pain is one of your best friends. If it were not for pain, you would not know that you were ill. You would not have time to gather your spiritual forces together to meet the intruder or to call the doctor.

Are you suffering from an acute disease? Then look to your physical habits—intemperance, indiscretions, tensions, and excesses. Perhaps your resistance is low. You may have neglected your body and are "running on the rims." The body requires care, exercise, rest, wholesome food, and fresh air. The man who neglects his body and the laws of physical health is likely to die suddenly, while the man who takes care of his body tends to die by imperceptible degrees. A natural deterioration which starts at birth should be the only occasion for death. It is all up to the individual. You cannot buy health, but you can prevent disease.

"But how about hereditary tendencies?" you ask. That is a good question. Hereditary physical traits and characteristics remain as tendencies only until mental indiscretions such as fear and worry set them in motion.

Jesus expressed the principle of psychosomatic medicine in the words, *"Whatsoever a man soweth that shall he also reap."* *Psychosomatic* refers to the soul-body relationship, *psyche*—meaning soul and *soma*—meaning *body*. Both the cause and the cure of disease are within man. When we understand this, we shall see that spiritual healing is a change from within. The cure is a threefold process:

1. Reversing destructive and discordant thoughts

2. Rebuilding the conscious mind upon a new foundation

3. Restoring the natural circulation of thought

Psychosomatic medicine transposes destructive mental and emotional conflicts into affirmations that remould our bodies according to the Divine Pattern. When the inner cases of disease have been destroyed and the subjective mind no longer denies our good, health begins to return.

Are you suffering from a chronic disease? Then look to your temperament. Like attracts like even in contagious diseases. To break down the body tissue, disease must be nourished by diseased thoughts. It cannot operate in any other way. To grow in the body, disease must find fertile soil.

Chronic disease does not come suddenly like acute disease. It must be built up through years of abnormal and indiscriminate thinking. That is why chronic diseases usually attack middle-aged people instead of youth. The chronic disease is an accumulation of perverse thinking that gradually weakens the structure of the body.

Chronic diseases can be prevented by a perfect relationship between the body and the soul. If disease is due to a lack of life or to the diversion of its currents to a destructive thought pattern or belief, health will return when the bottleneck is removed. It is true that flesh is subject to many ills, but disease cannot manifest while man is dwelling in a calm, peaceful, and temperate state of mind.

Acceptance of all that is implied in the words, *"Underneath are the everlasting arms,"* is the very foundation stone of the man who manifests his sense of security by his emotional control.

Contentment is an important factor in health. Discontented people are restless, irascible, unhappy people. They are filled with covetousness, dissatisfaction, despair, and friction. Wanting what they cannot have, they disturb the natural rhythm of the body and lay it open to disease.

Men in retirement have more chronic diseases than those who are daily occupied, for the retired man has too much time to think about himself and his ailments. "An untilled field runs to weeds." The energy once used in active work is now wasted. Having no outlet, it results in pent-up congestion. That is why the inactive person is harder to deal than the active one. The sick person who lives in idleness seldom recovers.

Out of pessimism come negation, privation, acid disposition, and rheumatism. Out of grief come waste, loss, and shrinkage. Out of melancholy comes tuberculosis. Out of monotony and unhappiness come high blood pressure, low blood pressure, and circulatory diseases. Out of parental confusion, contention, sex difficulties come childhood diseases—whooping cough, mumps, and chicken pox. If love and harmony were at work in the home and minds of parents, childhood diseases would be greatly lessened. Out of selfishness come congestion and colds. Out of anger come functional disturbances. Out of brooding comes heart trouble. Out of unhappiness come palsy and apoplexy. Out of grievances and resentment comes impaired vision. Out of pride comes acid in the blood. Out of despair comes kidney trouble. Out of moroseness comes liver trouble. Out of crabbedness comes indigestion. Out of egotism comes trouble in the spleen. Out of tension comes fatigue. Out of resignation come hopelessness and failure. Countless other reflexes are possible.

Do you find any of these abnormalities within yourself? Keep looking, and you may find others not mentioned here. You cannot share in the race consciousness and not find some. When you have found your specific physical irritation, reverse it, and the ailment will disappear with it. Plato said,

"All the mischiefs of the body proceed from the soul." That is why there can be no permanent healing of the body without a corresponding healing of the soul. Until the inward source of motivation has been dissolved, the disease will continue to appear. Like a prairie fire, it will break out first in one place and then in another.

"Why is it that some people heal more quickly than others?" one asks. Because of their optimism and their will to live. If there is no will to live, a person can die just as quickly from mumps as from nephritis. Optimism, on the other hand, accelerates healing, eases pain, and cleanses the blood.

Do you accept the dictum of three-score-years-and-ten? Then it becomes a law for you. The scientist says that you should live in your present body for at least five hundred years. You die before that time only because you live and think outside the law of God. Senility is nothing but an accumulation of irrational thoughts, apathy, indifference, inertia, and morbidity. Man eliminates himself by allowing his enthusiasm to grow dim. Old age is the penalty for losing faith in life. To live and think temperately will postpone senility for many years.

"But what about germs?" someone is sure to ask. That is another good questions. Germs are always present in the body, but they are only a secondary factor in disease. Something else must come first. If germs were a primary cause of disease, everyone would suffer in an epidemic.

"Why, then, are some people immune to germs and not others? Why do they attack at one time and not at another?" We shall answer both of these questions in one sentence. The quality of individual consciousness and the state of health determine the effect of harmful germs. Before germs can take hold, the cell resistance must be low. Immunity is not in the body but in the mind. When the mind is God-centered, germs have no place in which to breed. There is no spot in which they can take hold. When every part of the body is in right relation to every part, the body will express perfect health.

The old saw, "An ounce of prevention is worth a pound of cure," is still true. Unseating the mental causes of disease is just as important for the well person as for the sick one. The well person wants to keep his health, and the sick person wants to recover it. The well person analyzes the inner self to prevent disease, while the sick person analyzes the self to cure it. Health and sickness cannot occupy the mind and the body at the same time. Ease is irreconcilable with disease.

Some teachers would have us believe that all illness stems from mental reflexes, but this is not the case. There is, of course, no way of telling just how many diseases are of mental origin, but the following statements give us an indication. One doctor says that sixty per cent of his patients are sick because they do not know how to discipline and organize their emotions.

A famous clinic is authority for the statement that only twenty-five per cent of its cases can be handled by the instruments of science, the remaining seventy-five per cent being the result of sickness of the mind and soul.

Robert A. Russell

# Chapter V.   In Spite Of . . .
# Human Opinion

You cannot have read this far without realizing that true healing is spiritual. Indeed, you would not have chosen to read this book at all had you not been a searcher after Truth.

Again, if your bent is toward logic, toward order and arrangement, you will find the identification and discussion of the five steps in a treatment valuable. In this, as in any other learning, the beginner may be largely dependent upon his grasp of techniques, his understanding of mechanics, and his experience in seeing a process as a whole. As he progresses, he often finds that he is able to cut through a long process and achieve the same or a more perfect result. Many experienced drivers, excellent as they may be, find that they have forgotten even the names of the parts of the driving machinery that they handle so skillfully.

There is no one essential pattern for healing. Spiritual understanding is developed by many media, by many routes. The only thing important is that its development be continuous. "By their fruits, ye shall know them," said Jesus.

You may have by this time evolved a pattern of thought that is effective in spite of barriers, blockades, barricades, stumbling-blocks, obstacles, snags, curbs, and dampers. Or you may have developed a Faith (even so small as a grain of mustard seed) that will, according to St. Luke, cause a sycamine tree to obey you if you say, *"Be thou plucked up by the root and be thou planted in the sea,"* or which will, according to St. Matthew, remove a mountain at your command.

Of course, all bottlenecks are broken and healing is instantaneous if, despite external evidence, internal distress, and the sympathetic but adverse thought of those around one, he becomes conscious for a moment of his identity as living Spirit. In this case, time is not a factor; it serves in its true place as the everlasting Now.

This happy individual need read no further. He has become freed from the necessity of formal or pattern thinking. His spiritual intuition has been developed until it has become the mainspring of his life and living.

But for most of us, the search is an educative process. For those who wish to review the basic understandings on which spiritual healing is based, here is a brief catechism of eight questions and answers.

## SPIRITUAL HEALING

1.  How does one receive spiritual healing?

    Spiritual healing is based upon the Truth that every person is essentially perfect. In spite of all diseased appearances to the contrary, man is pure Spirit. This Spirit was never born, never gets sick, and never dies.

2.  What then needs to be healed?

    Nothing but the belief

3.  How does this healing affect the body?

    It permits a flow of life, unhampered by any discordant thought, mental reflex, inhibition, obstruction, pain, or limitation.

4.  What law does the spiritual therapist employ?

    The law of cause and effect.

5.   How does this law work?

Through it form is created by the image or idea.

6.   What are the requirements of spiritual healing?

That the one using the Principle rise above the images and ideas that produced the disease. No matter what the condition may be, he sick man must see himself as one with Living Spirit. He must contemplate the perfect Life now flowing through him and have absolute faith that it will instantly respond to him.

7.   How do we remove the mental cause of disease?

By bringing in the new concept of Truth and dwelling upon it until the old concept has been dissolved. *"Let Christ* [the Perfect Concept] *be formed in you."* That is, hold to it until it forms in you a consciousness of itself. Always start with the premise: "Perfect man, perfect God, and perfect Being." First, you find the mental cause that needs to be changed. Then you reverse it by bringing in the new and higher concept that transcends the lower. In other words, you convince your mind that this negative condition need not be. If Creative Power within us is continually remolding our bodies, to live and think on the affirmative and constructive side of life will bring out the perfection which we desire.

8.   Is there a Scriptural pattern for meeting the bottle-necks in human experience?

Yes. It is found in Proverbs 3:5;6.

*"Rely with all your heart on the Eternal and never lean on your own insight; have mind of him wherever you may go, and he will clear the road for you."**

---

* Moffatt translation.

When things get too thick for you, put your whole trust in God. *"Rely on the eternal with all your heart."* Take the initial step, and Spirit will go before you making clear, easy, and successful your way. Like a massive bull dozer, He will clear all the difficulties and obstacles for you.

# TREATMENT FOR HEALING

The process begins with your desire. (Recognition)

If you *know* that the very presence of your longing, your wish, your ambition, or your awareness of a better or a different way of living is certain proof that the condition or change you desire has at the moment a spiritual existence, your part in bringing it into reality on the physical plane will be greatly shortened.

Sharpen the outline of your desire to make a definite image or concept. Bring it out of a vague nebulous state; make it assume the proportions of reality.

The next step is to hold the picture you have made though meditation and silence until it forms in you a consciousness of itself. (Identification)

Then speak the word or declare what you desire. Imagine that Christ is actually present with you and speak the words with the authority, feeling, and tone that you think He would use in speaking them for you. (The Decree)

Sit quietly for five or ten minutes in what the author calls the Period of Acceptance, or Gestation. (Realization) Get very still and center your thought in the Presence of Christ. Feel His healing peace and power flowing through every nerve, muscle, organ, and tissue, cleansing, equalizing, and renewing everything unlike itself.

Conclude by thanking Him for the great healing that has already taken place and try to hold the power that has been released in you as you go about your other activities. (Release)

Do everything with ease and confidence and deliberation. Know that the treatment continues even after you leave the Silence. *"He that keepeth Israel neither slumbers nor sleeps."* Creative Power continues to work in your behalf even when you are busy with other things.

In this case the treatment is for healing. The pattern unfolded is applicable to any other condition which forms a bottleneck to spiritual growth or demonstration. In spite of bottlenecks, you Red Sea will part to give a free passage, your river of Jordan will be cut off, the manna will fall, the oil will be multiplied, the water will turn into wine, the net will be filled with a multitude of fishes, the storm will be stilled, the unclean spirit will come out, the fever will leave, the leprosy will depart, and you will be restored.

## STEP ONE. RECOGNITION

Start your healing treatment in the silence by saying to yourself with deep feeling:

I RECOGNIZE THAT GOD IS THE ONLY HEALING POWER THERE IS AND THAT IT IS RIGHT HERE WITHIN ME NOW.

I RECOGNIZE THAT ANYTHING UNLIKE GOD IS NOW DISSOLVED BY THE FULFILLMENT

OF MY WORD. I RECOGNIZE THAT THE SUBCONSCIOUS MIND (SOUL) CAN ONLY MATERIALIZE SUCH IMAGES AS HAVE BEEN DEEPLY AND FIRMLY INDUCED IN MIND AND HAT THE NEW CONCEPT IS THE LAW UNTO MY DESIRE.

I RECOGNIZE THAT THERE IS NO OBSTRUCTON TO THE OPERATION OF THIS NEW CONCEPT WHICH I AM NOW HOLDING IN MIND.

I RECOGNIZE THAT MY BODY IS CARRIED IN MY MIND AS AN IDEA WHICH OUT-PICTURES MY MENTAL ATTITUDE.

I RECOGNIZE THAT A CHANGE OF CONSCIOUSNESS WILL RESULT IN A CHANGE OF MY BODY. IF MY CONSCIOUSNESS HAS BEEN HOLDING AN IMAGE OF DISEASE IN MY BODY, A CHANGE OF CONSCIOUSNESS WILL AUTOMATICALLY WIPE OUT THE DISEASE. I RECOGNIZE THAT GOD RESPONDS TO ME BY CORRESPONDING TO MY STATES OF THOUGHT. I ENTER INTO HIS LIFE, PERFECTION, AND WHOLENESS IN SUCH DEGREE AS I COMPREHEND IT.

I RECOGNIZE THAT BEHIND, IN, AND THROUGH ALL DISEASE THERE IS AN INFINITE POWER AND INTELLIGENCE THAT RESTORES, CLEANSES, AND MAKES WHOLE.

I RECOGNIZE THAT THERE IS A PERFECT SELF AT THE CENTER OF MY BEING WHICH HAS NEVER BEEN TOUCHED BY AFFLICTION OR

DISEASE, AND THAT I CAN CALL IT FORTH
THROUGH MY RECOGNITION.

TO BE AWARE OF THIS PERFECT SELF IS TO
BE SAVED FROM WHATEVER I NEED TO BE
SAVED FROM.

I RECOGNIZE THAT DISEASE IS NOT REALITY
AND THAT IT HAS NO LAW TO SUPPORT IT.
IN MY SPIRITUAL BODY I AM NOW, ALWAYS
HAVE BEEN, AND ALWAYS WILL BE WHOLE
AND WELL.

I RECOGNIZE THAT MY PERFECTION AND
HEALTH AND WHOLENESS ARE MERELY
HIDDEN FROM ME BY MY FALSE BELIEF AND
THAT THE ONLY THING THAT HAS TO BE
HEALED IS MY BELIEF.

## STEP TWO. IDENTIFICATION

Since God is all life, my life is some part of God Life. There
being only Life, I must be identified and unified with this
Life. Where? In the subjective part of my mind. How do I
identify myself with this Life? How do I employ the energy
and vitality of God so that it flows through my body temple
as vibrant and perfect health? Through awareness.

To the degree that I become conscious of and feel the Presence
of Divine Life does it become an active force in my body. I
therefore make my decrees with acceptance and faith,
knowing that the Law responds to me by corresponding to
my word.

THE HEALING POWER OF CHRIST IS NOW ACTIVE IN ME AND I AM MADE WHOLE.

I NOW IDENTIFY MYSELF WITH GOD POWER WHICH HEALS EVERYTHING IN MY BODY THAT NEEDS HEALING AND BRINGS FORTH THE HIGHEST STATE OF PERFECTION WITHIN ME.

THE KINGDOM OF GOD IS A WELLSPRING WITHIN ME, AND I AM ALIVE WITH RADIANT HEALTH.

IDENTIFYING MYSELF WITH THE KINGDOM WITHIN ME, I HAVE ACCESS TO THE FULL POWER AND GLORY OF GOD. I AM RENEWED, REVITALIZED, RESTORED, STRENGTHENED, AND MADE VICTORIOUS. THE DIVINE PLAN OF BODILY ACTION IS NOW AT WORK WITHIN ME.

I IDENTIFY MYSELF WITH THE DIVINE PLAN WHICH INTERPRETS ITSELF TO ME THROUGH STRENGTH, POWER, AND BUOYANT HEALTH. EVERY CELL, ORGAN, AND FUNCTION OF MY BODY RESPONDS TO THE DIVINE ENERGY NOW FLOWING THROUGH ME.

I IDENTIFY MYSELF WITH THIS DIVINE ENERGY WHICH FLOWS THROUGH ME IN EVER-WIDENING CIRCLES OF HEALING. THE LESS BECOMES MORE, THE ISOLATION BECOMES INCLUSION, AND THE SEPARATION BECOMES ONENESS. THE ABNORMAL BECOMES NORMAL. WRONG ACTION BECOMES RIGHT ACTION.

THE QUICKENING, VITALIZING POWER OF SPIRIT FLOODS MY WHOLE BEING AND I AM RADIANT, VITAL, AND ALIVE.

IDENTIFYING MYSELF WITH THE ALL-PROVIDING POWER WITHIN ME MAINTAINS, SUSTAINS, RECREATES, AND KEEPS MY BODY IN PERFECT RENEWING ORDER. GOD'S LAW OF BALANCE KEEPS HEARTBEATS TRUE, BLOOD PURE, AND EVERY FUNCTION PERFECT AND HARMONIOUS.

AS A TEMPLE OF SPIRIT, MY BODY IS MADE OF DIVINE SUBSTANCE.

IDENTIFYING MYSELF WITH THE TEMPLE *"NOT MADE WITH HANDS, ETERNAL IN THE HEAVENS,"* I REALIZE THAT MY BODY IS NO LONGER SUBJECT TO PHYSICAL AND MATERIAL LAWS. IT IS GOVERNED ENTIRELY BY SPIRITUAL LAW.

I AM ONE WITH THE LIFE OF GOD. MY BODY IS FASHIONED AFTER THE LIKENESS OF THE DIVINE PATTERN.

IDENTIFYING MYSELF WITH THE LIFE AND ENERGY OF GOD DISSOLVES ALL PAIN AND DISCORD.

MY WHOLE BEING MANIFESTS THE EASE, HARMONY, PEACE, AND STRENGTH OF THE SPIRIT WHICH INDWELLS ME.

THE LIFE OF GOD NOW FILLS MY BODY TEMPLE
AND I AM HEALED AND MADE WHOLE.

IDENTIFYING MYSELF WITH THE ONE
SUBSTANCE OUT OF WHICH EVERYTHING IS
MADE, I CALL IT INTO ACTIVITY THROUGH
MY WORD. *"SPEAK THE WORD ONLY AND
MY SERVANT SHALL BE HEALED."* AS I SPEAK
THE WORD OF HEALING, DIVINE SUBSTANCE
IS RELEASED THROUGHOUT MY BEING. MY
BODY NOW OBJECTIFIES THE GOD IDEA
WHICH IS FOREVER PERFECT.

## Step Three. The Decree

*"Thou shalt also decree a thing, and it shall be established unto thee."*

*To decree* means to involve a word in thought, or to set a word in motion. This does not necessarily mean a word formed by sounds or letters; it may be a wordless mental concept. To *decree* or *declare* means to form, to make clear. A word begins with a matrix or mould in mind. It becomes flesh (takes form) throught Spiritual Substance. To speak the word is to decree that your concept shall be made flesh.

What is the new concept that you wish to substitute for the old concept of disease? By accepting the new, you nullify the old.

As an illustration let us use this one:

THE QUICKENING, VITALIZING POWER OF
SPIRIT RIGHT NOW IS RENEWING ME AND
RESTORING ME TO PERFECT HEALTH.

This is your intention. We shall refer to it as well as to other affirmations as *the word*. All affirmations converge in *the word*. *The word* is all the declarations of Truth in concentration, working through subjective Law. *"So shall my word be that goeth forth out of my mouth; it shall not return unto me void, but it shall accomplish that whereunto it is sent."*

## STEP FOUR. REALIZATION

"The worlds in which I live are two:
The world I am and the world I do."

--Henry Van Dyke

As we approach the next step, it might be well to define the word *realization*. It is from an old Sanskrit word which means "from — thought — to — thing." Realization is thus a subjective process which leads from the unseen to the seen, from decree to fulfillment, from thought to thing. It is a dual process which begins with a thought (the concept of the thing wanted) and then acts to materialize the object embodied in the thought. True realization is based upon this two-fold process. Failure to carry the process into action means a partial result or no result at all.

In its truest sense, realization means the same thing is actualization. It is, so to speak, Mind in precipitation, the word becoming flesh, the idea taking form. It is imperative, however, that the Decree, prayer, or treatment be followed by the action. Jesus said, *"Faith without works* [prayer without action] *is dead."* Complete realization is both choice and acceptance. It is convincing the inner mind that what we say is true.

The principal work in realization is to keep the body and mind relaxed and clear of tension, strain, confusion, contradictions, doubts, and anxieties. The object is to keep the healing Life of God flowing from the center of the being to the afflicted parts of he body, and to know that It is manifesting Itself in all that we think, say, and do. We must not only declare the truth about our bodies but must act and feel the truth of what we say. We must think and live in such a way that right action becomes the law of our being.

When we realize that our bodies respond to our word, there will no longer be anything for disease to act with. This realization is true not only of the malady which afflicts us but of our whole organism. Jesus understood and demonstrated the Law of Realization so perfectly that He needed only to say to the man sick of the palsy, *"Arise and walk."*

Metaphysically interpreted, realization is faith in form and acceptance objectified. The mind formulates an idea (representing the fulfillment of some need or desire) and then concentrates all its faculties and forces to make that idea real in the soul and in the outer world.

I REALIZE THAT THERE IS A LAW IN MY MIND WHICH IS NOW RELEASING INTO MY BODY EVERYTHING NECESSARY TO ITS WHOLENESS AND PERFECTION. THERE IS NO BARRIER TO THE OPERATION OF THIS CONCEPT.

THERE IS NO INACTION, OVERACTION, SUBNORMAL ACTION, OR ABNORMAL ACTION.

THERE IS NO BLOCKAGE, FRUSTRATION, PAIN, IRRITATION, INFLAMMATION, AGITATION, OR CONTRADICTION.

THERE IS NO BITTERNESS, CONGESTION, REPULSION, DISSENSION, INCOMPLETION, OR DEFLECTION.

THERE IS ONE PERFECT CIRCULATION FLOWING THROUGH MY BODY. IT IS NEVER CONGESTED, IMPEDED, POLLUTED, OR RETARDED.

THIS CIRCULATION IS STRONG, STEADY, VIGOROUS, AND FORCEFUL. IT AUTOMATICALLY DISSOLVES EVERYTHING THAT IS UNLIKE GOD.

AS THE SUN LIQUIFIES THE ICEBERG, SO MY CONSCIOUSNESS OF GOD'S PRESENCE LIQUIFIES ALL PAIN AND DISCORD. I KNOW THAT THE PERFECT LIFE OF GOD IN AND THROUGH ME IS NOW RECREATING MY BODY AFTER THE DIVINE PATTERN.

### Step Five. Release

The final and important step in the process is the release or planting of the word. If the seed is not planted (released), it cannot come to fruition. The word is the cause; healing is the effect. If the word is properly released within the mentality, there will be a definite answer. The law says that *"Whatsoever a man soweth that shall he reap."* The treatment moves from cause to effect in such degree as our consciousness embodies the idea.

Many students after giving a treatment say, "Now I shall leave it with God." That is good practice if you leave it with God but bad practice if you leave it to Him. The first attitude brings great success in spiritual work. The second attitude, on the other hand, scatters your good. *"If two of you shall agree on earth as touching any thing that they shall ask, it shall be done for them."* In the first attitude, God is working *with* you; in the second attitude, He is working *without* you. In leaving it to God, you are dividing your good because you are believing in duality. You are implying that God's activity and your activity are two separate activities. In other words, you are separating your activity from God's activity. *"The Father worketh hitherto and I work."* To leave it to God is not only to break your unity with God by assuming that His activity is something separate from your activity, but to evade your responsibility. In metaphysical language, you are following two powers instead of one, and you are headed for failure. Do you see the difference? When you leave it with God, your contact is maintained, and the work continues. You are with God and He is with you. *"As many as are led* [Practice the Presence] *by the Spirit of God, they are the Sons of God." "All things work together for good."*

The choice then is between activating the treatment (giving it continuity) by leaving it *with* God and neutralizing it by leaving it *to* God.

I CONSCIOUSLY RELEASE THIS WORD. I RELEASE ANY SENSE OF FALSE RESPONSIBILITY FOR MAKING IT HAPPEN. THIS I DO BY KNOWING THAT IT ACTIVATES THE LAW OF GOD-MIND, WHICH CAN ONLY ANSWER AFFIRMATIVELY TO THIS WORD AND DESIRE, BY COMPLETELY AND FULLY, AND WITH FEELING, ACCEPTING THIS WORD

TO BE THE TRUTH ABOUT ME IN GENERAL AND THIS CONDITION IN PARTICULAR. I CAN RELEASE IT WITHOUT STRAIN, DOUBT, OR ANXIETY. *"IT IS NOT I, BUT THE FATHER WITHIN, HE DOETH THE WORKS."*

I NOW REST THIS CASE. I THANK GOD FOR THE PERFECT FULFILLMENT OF MY DESIRE.

Another way to keep your word alive and working in your behalf is to lift up your heart each time the physical condition comes to your attention and say:

FATHER, I THANK THEE THAT THOU ART AT WORK ON THIS CLAIM NOW.

The answer may come immediately or it may take a long time. But the important thing is that you keep your courage and mental level high. Metaphysical treatments are cumulative in their effect, and *"Ye know not the hour when the Son of man cometh."* The success of the treatment will depend upon the continuity of your faith and expectancy. Since God is everywhere equally present, He is in every disease. To know this is to realize that the healing has already taken place.

I have observed this Law at work and I believe in it. Several years ago, a dear friend fell down a long flight of stone steps and was seriously injured. She was rushed to the hospital where she lay in a coma with a fractured skull and other serious injuries.

After three specialists in consultation had said the case was hopeless, I was called to the hospital by a member of the family.

The night nurse told me as I entered the room that the patient could not live through the night—that the doctors had given her up.

"Given her up!" I said. "What do you mean?"

"There's no hope for her. She will probably die in the night," she responded.

"Aren't doctors the sworn enemies of death? What right have they to 'give up' a woman who is still alive?" I demanded.

There was a strong atmosphere of despair and resignation all through the room; and as I sat beside the patient's bed, I asked the nurse if she would mind leaving the room while I prayed.

"Not at all," she replied and stepped quietly out into the hall.

This was a crisis. I knew that I had to furnish God with a clear and open channel to work though. A great sense of peace filled me as I entered the Silence and began to pray for the speedy recovery of the patient. There was no response from her at first. Reaching through the rail on the side of the bed and taking the woman's hand in mind, I said,

"GOD, WE ARE NOT GOING TO LET THIS WOMAN DIE. SHE HAS MANY USEFUL YEARS AHEAD OF HER YET, AND WE WANT HER TO LIVE. WE ARE ASKING YOU RIGHT NOW TO TOUCH THIS BROKEN AND BRUISED BODY AND TO RESTORE HER TO PERFECT HEALTH AND WHOLENESS. WE BELIEVE THAT YOU ARE RELEASING THE HEALING POWER OF JESUS CHRIST IN HER THIS INSTANT AND THAT IT IS POWERFUL ENOUGH TO

PENETRATE AND DISPEL EVERY NEGATIVE
AND INHARMONIOUS CONDITION."

Did she live? Of course she lived. Before the prayer was finished, she had regained consciousness. She turned to me saying, "Why, Dr. Russell, what are you doing here at this time of night?" It was truly a resurrection. On the second day after my visit, she was taken for a drive.

Now suppose that I had surrounded patient with fear thoughts, and had wrapped her around with a defeatist attitude instead of seeing the radiant Life and imperishable Power that was hers despite the evidence of the physical senses? I do not have to tell you how different the result would have been.

# Chapter VI.   In Spite Of . . .
## Handicaps

"This is my fourth Christmas in bed and it doesn't look as though I will ever get out."

"My arthritis has gotten so bad that I have had to give up my painting."

"Rheumatic fever has left me with a bad heart and the doctor says that I can never work again."

"My eyesight has grown so poor that I must give up my studies."

"Polio has left me a hopeless cripple."

"I have lost my leg, and I can't see any reason for going on."

"This war wound has ruined my life and my hopes."

"It is useless to try any longer. My job demands a first-rater; I am only a second-rater."

"It is impossible to make this adjustment. I am utterly discouraged."

"Alcohol has gotten the best of me. I can't fight any longer."

"I started out with great possibilities, but fear and self-consciousness have ruined my chances."

"I have been denied the normal family relationships. My life is barren and empty."

*"In the world,"* said Jesus, *"ye shall have tribulation but be of good cheer; I have overcome the world."* In the world you will have handicaps, but be of good cheer. There is a way out of them. If it is true that "misery loves company," we should find consolation in the fact that handicaps are the common lot of all mankind. Everyone has a drawback of some kind. Some are visible to the world; others are known only to the individual.

How did you get where you are today? If you are dissatisfied with your present status and realize how far you are from where you should be, you are quite likely to say that you are where you "because of" your handicaps.

But if you can see growth in yourself, if you have achieved to the extent that you find satisfaction in living despite your awareness of an ideal yet to be reached, you will probably be proud to say that you are accomplishing your purpose "in spite of" handicaps.

It is not the handicap that determines our success or failure in life; it is the way we meet it—it is our reaction to it. The real problem is not the deformity itself, but the way in which the deformity affects the total personality.

Franklin D. Roosevelt arrived at the highest office in the land "in spite of" the dread disease of polio. Lionel Barrymore, the incomparable movie actor, continued his acting in a wheel chair when he became so crippled with arthritis that he could no longer stand or walk.

Call the role of the noble handicapped who have won fame and positions of power in spite of their deficiencies, and you will find that in every case the secret of their victory was in their minds. They not only refused to submit to their handicaps, but they also learned how to use them.

Did epilepsy stop Socrates, Richelieu, or Napoleon? Did crippling infirmities stop Robert Louis Stevenson? Did blindness stop Homer, Milton, Fanny Crosby? Did a club foot stop Sir Walter Scott or Lord Byron? Did deafness stop Beethoven? Did defeat after defeat stop Balzac? Did paralysis stop Louis Pasteur? Did rebuffs stop Schumann-Heink? Did a bad heart and crippled limbs stop Charles Steinmetz? Did the loss of a lung stop Roger Babson? Did physical infirmity stop Admiral Byrd? Did repeated failures and criticism stop Walt Disney? Go on and name hundreds more. What does it take to stop a man? Nothing but his admission of defeat. Defeat and victory are both in the mind. No man can be defeated until he accepts defeat.

In Mexico, there is a famous statue by Jesus Garcia called "In Spite Of." It is a monument to the dauntless who have succeeded in spite of their handicaps. When the sculptor was well on the way with his statue, he lost his right hand. To most sculptors, this would have been a supreme tragedy, but not to Garcia. Undaunted by the calamity that had befallen him, he learned to carve with his left hand and finished the statue. There is much wisdom in the statement: "When Fate throws a dagger at you, there are two ways to catch it: either by the blade or by the handle."

The law of averages says that there is just so much trouble in the world and that every man must take his share. "But that isn't true," you say. "There are some people who have more trouble than others," and more often than not you say, "But I have more trouble than others." That point of view is an optical illusion. The reason you think that some people have more trouble than others is that you see them at the critical periods in their lives and not as a whole. The reason you think that you have more trouble than others is that in your times of distress you tend to forget your blessings.

It is not uncommon to hear people say, "Why did this have to happen to me?" The answer is that you are part of the race consciousness. In the race consciousness, there is no security or immunity from hazards. Life is filled with them. You can start out from your home in the morning and be struck down by a car on the street. A deadly germ can get into your blood and all the skill of medical science be unable to avert the end. You can fall on the stairs in your home and become a life-long cripple.

Human life is filled with danger, jeopardy, misfortune, and peril. It has always been this way, and it will continue to be so until we learn how to live above the race consciousness, until we accept the Presence of God. *"In Christ Jesus ye are above the law and not subject to it."* So long as we are in the world, it behooves us to learn how to meet the world.

There is a story in the Gospel of St. Luke of a woman who had suffered from a proclivity in her back for eighteen years. The physician does not go into detail about the woman's trouble except to say that she was *"bowed together"* and could not stand up straight, but he does say that she had a *"spirit of infirmity."* What does that mean? It means that she had let her deformity distort her spirit. There was an emotional factor in her trouble that was even worse than the handicap itself. This emotional factor could have been self-consciousness, self-pity, or any one of a dozen other things; but whatever it was, it had brought her great mental anguish and pain.

Here is a clear case of psychosomatic sickness. Jesus called the woman to him and said unto her, *"Woman, thou art loosed from thine infirmity. And He laid His hands on her; and immediately she was made straight and glorified God."* Now note the method of healing that Jesus employed in this case. First, he loosed the *"spirit of infirmity."* Then her body was made straight. Why didn't Jesus start with the woman's body? Because the source of her trouble was in her soul.

Do you see what destructive, emotional conflicts can do the body? Listen to the men of science. One doctor says, "I have treated many a patient with a broken leg when the more demanding need was to heal a broken heart." Another says that full half the people that crowd his offices have nothing wrong with them physically. What does the Mayo clinic mean when it reports that of 15,000 ulcer patients, eighty per cent were found not to have any physical cause for ulcer of the stomach? They mean that eight persons out of ten were suffering from emotional disturbances. The great Dr. Paul Du Bois said, "Religious faith is the best preventive against the maladies of the soul, mind, and body, and it is the most powerful medicine we have ever discovered for curing them." Be careful, however, what religious faith you choose. Make sure that it is sane, scientific, practical, and down to earth. Why does the author sound this warning? Because of the countless victims of irrational, nerve-shattering, misleading, and spurious religions whom he has found in mental institutions. Is it any wonder that psychiatrists will not allow ministers to discuss religion with their patients in these hospitals? How much better for humanity it would be if clergymen and their doctrines were screened by state boards of intelligent clerics before they were allowed to preach. One with a back *"bowed together"* does not need to be threatened with being toasted over the flames of an imaginary hell. He needs something constructive that will transform and fortify him within. If the representatives of the church do not teach mankind how to meet the vicissitudes of human existence, who will?

Rational religion says, "Make your handicap into an asset. Do something with it. Make something out of it." Irrational religion says, "Your handicap is a punishment from God. You have offended Him and He is wreaking vengeance upon you. You must suffer until you expiate your sin."

But how does the exponent of the latter point of view reconcile his views with the promise *"I [Jesus] am come that ye might have life and have it more abundantly"?* Or with the statement of St. Paul, *"My strength is made perfect in weakness . . . . I take pleasure in infirmities, . . . . for Christ's sake: for when I am weak, then I am strong"?* And with his inquiry, *"If ye then being evil know how to give good gifts unto your children, how much more shall your Father which is in Heaven give good things to them that ask him?"* Since God is all Life and all Love, how can Life and Love create anything unlike itself? How can it inflict punishment or disease? The truth is that disease has only the power over us which we give it. Which is better — to make something out of our infirmities or to fold up and die under them? Whom are you worshipping — the vindictive, tribal God of Moses, or the triumphant, loving God of Jesus? The first brings captivity and defeat. The second brings freedom and success.

Sidney Powell[*] tells a story of determination worth reading. "When Fred Stone crashed while piloting his airplane and sustained injuries that almost seem to exhaust the catalogue — compound fracture of the left ankle, compound fracture of the shin, fracture of the right thigh, fracture of two ribs on one side and three on the other side, dislocation of the shoulder,

---

[*] Powell, Sidney, *Life's High Hurdles.* Abingdon-Cokesbury Press.

scalp injury requiring twenty stitches, broken jaw, tongue bitten almost in two — the doctor told him he might possibly walk again some day, but to appear on the stage in such parts as he had played during his whole previous career was impossible. But as a boy nine years old, he had mastered the high wire; he had showed a dogged determination to refuse to give up a thing until he had mastered it. He says, 'That was probably just the natural desire to try myself out against things, but it is why I came to be an acrobat.' And it was the reason why, three years after the doctors had prophesied that he could never appear again as an acrobat, he was back on the stage in a new show."

Dauntless Christ-conscious men are like airplanes. They rise not with the wind but against it. Normal Peale in telling the story of Harold Russell[*] gives us a sentence to remember. "Who is Harold Russell? He is a famous actor. Before the war he was a clerk in a meat market. In the army he made quite a little progress. But one day he picked up some kind of explosive and lost both hands. After a while they fixed him up with artificial hands which he calls 'hooks' — 'the same kind of hooks they used to have in the meat market,' he remarked. Had he not had a normal mind this would have filled him with gloom. But Russell said to himself, 'It is not what a man has lost that matters, but what he has left.' It seemed only a matter of months when Harold Russell became one of the motion picture stars in 'The Best Years of Our Lives.'"

You may forget this story in years to come, but it is important that you remember the truth which it contains: *"It is not what a man has lost that matters, but what he has left."* The outcome of every handicap depends upon your attitude toward it. If it gets you, you are lost. If you get it, you are saved.

---

[*] Used by permission of the author.

*"How long halt ye between two opinions?"* asked Elijah. Ask yourself, "What am I going to do about my handicap? What am I going to make of it? Am I going to make it an ally or a hindrance, an asset or a liability?" The place to decide this issue is in the mind and soul. If there is no handicap in the soul, there will be none in the body.

A handicap may be mental, physical, or emotional. It may be a poor memory, a twisted limb, or an uncontrollable temper. To some people, a handicap is an excuse for quitting, for hiding, for lying down, or giving up. To others, it is a challenge to conquer, to turn the clouds inside out, to make their difficulties serve them. No one can be blamed for his handicap, but he should be blamed for not making something out of it.

One does not overcome handicaps by resignation and despair but by seeing the blessing in them. The Swedish people have a saying, "Blessed is he who sees a dawn in every midnight." The dawn is there, but it awaits recognition.

There are two kinds of handicapped people in the world — the *out-going* and the *in-driving*. The outgoing personality turns to service toward others; the indriving turns toward self. The first leads to freedom; the second leads to neurosis. Self-centeredness is an enemy to health. The egocentric person is usually sick. Does that sound like preaching? Then listen to William James, the philosopher, who said, "The deepest drive of human nature is to be appreciated." If you are self-centered, you haven't time to think of anybody but yourself. The cure is to let yourself alone. Be *outgoing*. Get interested in other people whether you feel like it or not. They, too, need encouragement and appreciation. Give yourself and spend yourself. It won't cost you anything, and it will do you a world of good. Self-concern breeds emotional illness.

An old story gives the secret of overcoming self-centeredness as knowing and using the fact that "Everybody's lonesome," Jesus said, *"He that loseth his life shall find it."* In effect, he was saying "Lose the self, and you will lose your ills." While Alexander Bell was trying to build a hearing aid for his wife's deafness, he invented the telephone. When Abraham Lincoln lost himself in the cause of emancipation and the relief of human suffering, he immortalized himself.

Hugh MacNair Kahler* tells the story of two northern doctors who went to a southern village to die. One was tubercular, the other arthritic.

The author aroused the interest of each in the other, and the man who would not take a fighting chance for himself took it for a fellow physician. Each brought his best skill to bear on the other's case, with the result that both lived and became loved and influential residents of the town. Kahler concludes: "Each of them in private conversation with me always took credit for having helped the other to live those nineteen extra years of useful life. Each in public and in private gave the other credit for having cured him. Neither one . . . . ever suspected that in his self-forgetting effort to help the other, each had cured himself."

The metaphysician says, "Face your liability. Make something of it." How? By being bigger than your disability. When you know the nature of your handicap, you will know how to meet it. The people who never rise above their handicaps are the people who try to conceal them or to use them for little personal ends. We refer, of course, to the coward, the sympathy-seeker, and to those who use their handicaps as an

---

* Kahler, Hugh MacNair. "Drama in Everyday Life." *Reader's Digest,* April, 1944.

excuse for laziness. To face your handicap, on the other hand, is half the battle. Dr. William Osler said, "We are not likely to die of a disease which we know we have and which we are watching, but rather of a disease that takes hold unexpectedly because we are not prepared." Most of us are very honest with ourselves about our abilities but are inclined to be very dishonest about our limitations. It is important to analyze our handicaps and to see them as they are. In fact, it is only as we recognize and analyze our handicaps that we can discover what can be done with them. Ask yourself these questions:

1.  What is the nature of my handicap?

2.  Is there anything about it than can be altered?

3.  Is there anything about it that cannot be changed?

When you find the factors that cannot be changed, resolve to accept them. Accept them with your whole being and promise yourself that you will never fight nor resist them again. This is the first step in turning your liability into an asset and the first step in removing the tension from your problem. The next step is to surrender what still seems unalterable to God who, as the Psalmist says . . . . *"daily beareth our burden."* When man lets go, God takes hold.

Do you see the picture clearly? Before you can use your handicap and make something out of it, you must first recognize it. You change what you recognize as being changeable within your present understanding; what you have not the power to see as changeable you turn over to God, knowing that your vision and your faith will grow to encompass any difficulty. But how does one change the alterable factors in his situation? By substitution and compensation. The stream of life is just as irresistible and undefeatable as a stream of water. If it is obstructed in one place, it will find an outlet in another place. So it should be with you and with your physical, mental, and emotional bottlenecks. If you are hindered in one direction, you can work in another. If you are disabled in one ability, you can develop another. I know a woman who compensated for a terrible facial deformity by developing a brilliant mind. In fact, her lectures were so scintillating, stimulating, and transforming that the listener never thought of her face. She determined to carry on "in spite of" her deformity and became one of the most popular and sought after women in this country. "Don't give in to your handicap," says this intrepid soul, "but use it." Though every thing may be against you and though every way may be closed except up, God opens a way on your level where there is no seeming way. No barrier is impassable if you are determined to win.

Glenn Cunningham's story* bears this out. "When Glenn Cunningham was seven years old, he was so badly burned in a schoolhouse fire In Kansas that he lay helpless for weeks— his legs swathed in bandages. His right leg became crooked and shortened by two and one-half inches, pulled up at the knee by scar tissue. There were no toes on his left foot, and the arch had collapsed. The doctors said he would never be able to walk again, but he determined not only to walk but to run as well. He massaged his legs, and the family pulled them, although it caused him a great deal of pain. Soon he began to walk—at first with crutches and at the age of eleven without them. It hurt him to walk, but he found that when he ran he forgot the pain; and everywhere he went, he ran. Thus he developed his legs so that in his junior year in high school he made the track team; and in 1934 at Princeton's Palmer Stadium, Cunningham, representing the University

---

* Powell, Sidney — *Op. Cit.*

of Kansas, beat Bill Bonthrou of Princeton by forty yards and established the world's indoor mile record."

What is your handicap? You are the only one who can answer this question.

What is the technique for dealing with it? There are three ways in which you can overcome it.

1. You can transmute it through substitution and compensation by turning your energies in another directions.

2. You can eliminate it by facing yourself as you are and accepting the challenge which the handicap brings.

3. You can accept it by changing your thought about it (refusing to feel sorry for yourself, refusing to rebel, refusing to be negative in your attitude toward it).

Many rules have been given for overcoming handicaps, but they can all be summed up in the injunctions — *Establish the right attitude toward life*. There must not only be an analysis of the problem but also a grim determination to do something about it. Bemoaning our fate and dwelling in the thought of how wonderful things might have been is no solution. We must be realistic and intelligent. If there is a grace that is sufficient for us, we must find it and put it to work.

Let the handicapped say to himself: "Am I the only one who has to make the best out of second bests? Is my infirmity unique?" The answer is certain and comforting. The surest thing in all the world in addition to death and taxes is that everyone has a handicap. Yes, even those who are not aware of them. Did Joseph want to be sold into slavery, betrayed, lied about, and imprisoned? No! But he made something out of it. He turned the tables on his brothers; he changed an injury into a blessing.

Did Paul want a thorn in the flesh? You know by his prayer that he did not. What then did he say about it? *"My strength is made perfect in weakness.* [I will make something out of it.]" *"When I am weak I am strong."* Do you see what we mean by the positive attitude? History is made by the people who accept the challenge of the impossible and the incurable and drive throught to victory "in spite of everything."

Dr. Fosdick* tells this pertinent story:

"Do you hear the shouting in the Assembly Hall of the great Midwestern University? It is graduation day and there has never been such cheering — not even at a football victory — as greeted a crippled boy carried in the arms of his companions across the platform. Four years before, that boy had answered. 'Present' at the first roll call of his class.

'Stand up,' said the professor.

'I should like to, sir, but I have not been able to stand up since I was four years old.'

"But by being what he was in a difficult situation, that boy made such an impression on the University that, when his companions carried him up for his diploma, the great assemblage broke into such cheers as that college generation had not heard before."

---

* Fosdick, Harry Emerson, *The Power To See It Through.* Harper Brothers.

There are basic principles which you can learn and apply, principles that help you emerge victorious "in spite of" handicaps.

## 1. Do Not Compromise With Truth.

Do you remember the words of the three young men who were about to be thrown into the fiery furnace? *"The God whom we serve is able to deliver us from the burning furnace and from our power . . . But if not, know yet that we will not bow down before the golden image."* Note the words, "but if not." Our faith in God is not based upon the healing of our physical infirmities, the straightening of bent backs, or the restoration of withered hands although God can do that too. God did not save Jesus from the cross, but throught the cross, He saved the world. If our faith is strong enough and big enough, God will straighten the back. "But if not," we shall go straight on. There is a spiritual order in divine healing; to miss that order is to miss the blessing.

Since human afflictions are more mental than physical, the proper approach to healing is through the mind. What we need first is freedom from the power that the handicap holds over us. Our faith must be kept intact. The answer to prayer is secondary, but faith is primary. You can't trust God wholly "because of" what He does for you. You must trust Him "in spite of" the things you ask for that are not yet objectified for you on the material plane.

## 2. Do Not Compare Yourself With Other People.

If you say, "Handicapped as I am, I can never be like John Smith," you are playing a losing game. The wonderful thing about creation, is that you are not supposed to be like anyone else. Your only responsibility is to meet your handicap as superbly as you can. Say to yourself "I, John Jones, do here and now accept my handicap and with the help of God resolve to make something out of it."

### 3. CULTIVATE CONTENTMENT.

St. Paul said, *"I have learned in whatsoever state I am, therewith to be content"*; he had learned how to meet things as they came. Many people are overburdened mentally and physically because they try to meet their troubles in battalions. In most instances, difficulties arise one by one and should be met in single file just as the Bank Teller receives the customers in front of his window. It requires skill to do this, but developing the skill pays large dividends.

### 4. LET GO OF THE PAST.

*Yesterday* died last night. *Today* was born this morning. The Eskimos believe that they begin a new life with each new morning. Sleep for them is death. Waking is resurrection. If we could all get this realization, it would not only break our bondage to the past but would keep us eternally new and young. Age is a belief in time—the weight of years. To live outside of time (in the *now*) would mean continuous rejuvenation. Does that sound fantastic? Consider the statement that no one is more than a year old physically. If the mind does not grow old, the mind of a man of eighty is the same age as that of boy twelve. Where, then, do age and wrinkles come from? From our belief in time. If we could live and think in the present, the body would daily be renewed. Perhaps that is why St. Paul told us to be *"Be transformed by the renewing of the mind."* When the mind is renewed, the body is automatically transformed.

## 5. MAGNIFY YOUR ASSETS.

The reason many handicapped persons go down in defeat is that they take a negative view of life. They allow their deformities to hold the spotlight in consciousness instead of giving it to their assets. Perhaps these people do not realize that despondency is just as much of a disease as appendicitis. What the despondent person needs is to find the good and encouraging things in his situation and to magnify those. Jesus said *"Let your light . . . . shine."* Let the good come to the forefront of consciousness and crowd the bad out.

## 6. SURRENDER YOUR HANDICAP TO GOD.

If you keep your handicap bottled up within yourself, it will affect your whole life. If you try to deal with it yourself, you will make it worse. The only satisfactory way to handle it is to get it out of your hands and into God's Hands. Your power plus God's power can make something out of it. Are you brooding over your infirmity? Then you are trying to handle it by yourself. You can hand it back to God by thanking Him for the good that He is bringing out of it. Remember that miracles happen in a thankful heart.

## 7. BE WILLING TO CHANGE YOUR PLAN.

When things do not turn out the way you planned, be willing to try something else. Your success in life depends not upon one plan but upon your resiliency and flexibility in meeting changes. A friend of mine believed that he should have been a lawyer, but reverses made it necessary for him to quit school and he turned to another field. He became one of the most successful boys' leader in this country. It is a mistake to hold your plans too tenaciously. Flexibility is just as important to me as it is to trees. The rigid man is easily broken. The flexible man always comes back. Change is a law of growth.

## 8. Don't Trouble Trouble.

There is an old jingle which says, "Don't trouble trouble until trouble troubles you." In other words, do not anticipate trouble. Because you have had one heart attack is no reason for living in the expectation of having another. You can easily bring another on, however, by anticipating it in your thought. People perpetuate their ills from one day to another by anticipation. If you provide for failure, you will fail. If you provide for your handicap to get the upper hand, it will get the upper hand. If you provide a constructive channel for it, it will cease to be a liability. St. Paul said. *"But put ye on the Lord Jesus Christ, and make no provision for the flesh to fulfill the lusts thereof."*

## 9. Don't Pity Yourself.

Most handicapped persons are tempted to feel sorry for themselves. Self-pity leads to introversion, and introversion leads to despair. Self-pity is an emotional poison. It not only infects the entire personality, but it delays healing. It is a wise person who keeps his mental and emotional wounds clean.

## 10. Do Not Syndicate Your Troubles.

The first and most important thing in dealing with trouble is to unseat the pain by getting the trouble out into the open. Trouble is like a boil. When you lance it by discussing it with an understanding friend, you let out the poison. You whittle it down to size, and there is great relief.

There is a vast difference, however, between sharing your trouble and syndicating it. If you retail your trouble to everybody you meet, you increase the infection and your trouble grows. Syndicating your troubles is the quickest way to repel your fiends.

## 11. Don't Resist Your Trouble.

If you fight your trouble, it will fight back. Like any other difficulty, trouble grows through attention. The more you fight the more tense you become. The proper way to handle it is to agree with it. *"Agree with thine adversary quickly,"* said Jesus. Shift the center of gravity. Forget yourself by doing some constructive work for others. When you fight handicaps, when you think only of your own deliverance, you go down instead of up, backward instead of forward. The way to keep the healing power of God flowing through you is to remove tension and strain from your mind.

## 12. Find Something Interesting To Do.

The best medicine for introversion is interesting work. Work is one of the greatest healing agencies in life. Work is more than a blessing; it is a restorative. Without work, man has no incentive or design for living. The busy man has no time for self-pity, for disappointment, or for regrets. There are important things on his mind; he must be up-and-doing, growing, planning, climbing, exploring, selling, and creating. It is a wonderful thing to greet each new day with the realization that you have an important job to do. It doesn't matter whether the job is large or small, do as much or as little as you can and be happy and thankful to it. "But I am confines to my bed," someone says. So what? There are many useful and interesting occupations that you can pursue from your bed. Let the bedridden one say, "I may be shut in but I am not shut out."

## 13. IF YOU MUST DIE, DIE QUIETLY.

Since everyone is going to live forever, we might just as well begin now. Jesus said, *"This is life external,"* and He did not mean disease, decrepitude, or disintegration. He meant health, youth, wholeness, and perfection. Adjust yourself to the endless side of life, and you will arrest stagnation and inertia. Eternality is written in your inward parts, but you must practice it. Life always responds to what you see and feel. Open yourself to this Life within. Begin to live. "Growing old gracefully" is an impossibility. Grace and wrinkles do not go together. Metaphysically interpreted, "growing old gracefully" means to die easily — imperceptibly, without pain or disease. In the Divine Order, death is a translation and not a fight. Are you old, tired, and full of misery? Then you are not living life to the full. John Doe (personality) is not our life: God is. Know it, realize it, think it, live it, and practice it twenty-four hours a day. Think of the Life Force within you as boundless river forever flowing.

Sir Thomas Buxton said: "The longer I live, the more I am certain that the great difference between men, between the great and the insignificant, is energy, invincible determination, an honest purpose once fixed, and then death or victory. This quality will do anything in the world; and no talents, no circumstances, will make a two-legged creature a man without it."

Accepting his Power as our own, we shall rejoice with the psalmist, *"The lines are fallen unto me in pleasant places; yea, I have a goodly heritage."*

# Chapter VII.   In Spite Of . . .
## Marital Difficulties

"We don't agree about anything any more except the fact that we want a divorce."

"I can earn a better living than he can."

"My wife is a mess. I can't even recognize in her the girl I married."

"He's so crude."

"She doesn't understand me."

"All I want is peace."

If words were permanently recorded in the place in which they were spoken, the walls of the study of any minister today would reverberate unceasingly with expression such as these. Ministers the world over are attempting to meet their challenge in one way or another.

"Just a minute, please," I say to the one before me at the moment. "Not so fast. Let us try to get to the bottom of your trouble. You think now that divorce is the end. Let's look at it and think beyond it.

"Divorce is just another name for failure. It is a disastrous and disruptive step.

"When you too stood at the altar, you took each other 'for

better or for worse' until death parted you. You said, 'I do.' Now you are saying 'I don't.' Why this reversal of your decision? Did you go into your marriage with reservations? Was it consciously tentative? Were you leaving a loophole? And now are you going to violate the most sacred vows that any man and woman can take?

"Have you considered divorce in all it's many ramifications? Do you know what broken homes are like? Do you know what divorce can do to your life as well as to the lives of your children?"

"But there is no other way," says the grieving, or indignant, or self-righteous individual.

"Then face the facts!" I say. "Your divorce will keep pulling you back to face our failure. It will not only put a temporary stigma on you and on your home and children, but it will influence your whole life adversely. Marriage is a union of two persons; in it there is no room for the development of one individual at the expense of the other."

"What are the factors that have brought your marriage to this sorry pass?" I ask the wife who comes before me. To make her come alive to you, shall we give her a name? Helen, or Phyllis, or Catherine? Let it be Helen in this instance. Of course, the cases discussed are so typical that you can name the characters yourself. Some few of you may find yourselves in the case histories given.

"How long have you lived with your husband?" (Shall he be Jerry?)

"Six years."

"Do you have any children?"

"A little boy."

"Have you considered him in this step? How are you going to divide him between you? You can't cut him in half, you know, and a boy needs a father just as much as he does a mother."

"I'm really thinking most about him. He'd be better off without his father."

"Do you go to church?"

"No."

"Does your husband go to church?"

"No."

"Why not?"

"Because he is a Roman Catholic and I am a Presbyterian." (Or, "Because we are tired on Sunday." Or "Because there are so many other things to do.")

"Do you have family prayers? Do you say grace at your meals? Is there any spiritual atmosphere in your home?"

"No."

"Well, what are the other factors that have brought you to this momentous decision?"

"My husband drinks too much. He will not face his responsibilities."

"What do you mean by that?"

"He is selfish, indifferent, and irresponsible. He thinks only of his own pleasure. I have told him time and time again that I do not like drinking in our home, but he insists on having cocktail parties every week end."

"Do you drink?"

"Not unless I have to. When we were first married, I toured the taverns with him. Now I find that he is dating a young woman who works in his office, I know that he sometimes stays out with her two and three in the morning."

"How do you know this?"

"I have had him shadowed."

"Did you ever remonstrate with him about this?"

"Yes, I did."

"What did he say?"

"That I was old-fashioned."

"Then you accuse him of disloyalty?"

"I certainly do."

"What else do you find wrong with him?"

"He give so little time to his family. He spends his evenings on work that he brings home from the office and spends weeks ends fishing, golfing, or skiing."

"What does he do on Sunday?"

"He reads the paper, eats, and sleeps."

"Does he ever take you out for recreation?"

"Seldom since our son was born."

"What other factors have influenced you in your decision?"

"My husband is careless and untidy. He never hangs up his clothes and never puts the top on the shaving soap. He drops cigarette ashes on the carpets and furniture and leaves his golf clubs on the floor."

"Have you every prayed for your husband?"

"I certainly have without any result. I cannot take this mental cruelty any longer."

Have you followed this case closely? Then put yourself in my place and write down on paper just exactly what you would say to this young wife in an effort to get her to change her mind about divorce. She has her suitcase packed for Reno, and you will have to clinch your arguments on the spot if you are to stop her.

Have you finished? Then let us go to the case of a young husband — Jim. Let us hear his story:

"I blew up yesterday, and it looks as though Margaret and I will have to go our separate ways."

"Why?"

"Because I have taken all that one man can be expected to take. I have tried to straighten my wife out but it's no use. She doesn't seem to care about me or her home."

"Is she interested in some other man."

"Not that I know of."

"Then what is wrong with her?"

"She is careless and shiftless. All she wants to do is play canasta and bridge with her college friends. She lies in bed all morning and plays cars all afternoon. I get my own breakfast. The house is always dirty, the beds are seldom made, and the sink is usually filled with dirty dishes. My dinners are prepared in a hurry and come mostly from cans. I may be a crank on the subject, but it is my contention that a wife owes something to her husband. If Margaret were ill or incapacitated in any way, there might be some excuse for her lying in bed until noon. But she is healthy, strong, indifferent, and lazy."

"Have you ever discussed her faults with her?"

"Yes I have, and the discussion always leads to a family row. Her folks had plenty of money when she was growing up, and she never had to do anything around the house."

"What else do you find wrong with her?"

"Her temper and inquisitiveness. She flies off the handle without any provocation and always has to know everything about my affairs. She opens all my mail and wants to make all the important decisions in our home. She refuses to entertain my friends because she does not like them."

"Then you feel that there is no basis for the future of your marriage?"

"I certainly do. I am so fed up with the whole thing that I cannot take it any more."

All right, students, get out your pencil again and see if you can work out a solution to this problem. What would you say in this young husband to save his marriage? What are the factors involved? What therapy would you apply? We could recite many other case histories but these two are so typical that they will help us analyze this special area of difficulty. Now put what you have written away until you reach the end of the chapter.

It is a sad commentary on our educational system that so little thought and time has been given to the preparation of young people for marriage which, after all, is one of the most important institutions in the world. We train our young people for practically everything in life except marriage. When young persons are taught how to make happy and successful adjustments in marriage, the divorce rate will go down.

There are some psychiatrists who contend that sexual maladjustment is the most frequent cause of divorce, but statistics do not support such a theory. The real problem is not physical incompatibility but psychic incompatibility. The problem is one of personal relationships and mutual understanding. The things that vitiate marriage vitiate life. Rabbi Brickner said, "Success in marriage is much more than finding the right person: it is a matter of being the right person." In fact, it is a matter of two persons making themselves right for each other.

It is not the institution of marriage that is under an oxygen tent today; it is the partners in marriage. They rush to the altar with no preparation and no understanding of each other. Before marriage, they are confident that their great love will solve all their problems. When the honeymoon is over and the glamour has worn off, they begin to wonder if they have made a mistake. Everything was glorious during the courtship, but now they find that all is not what it seemed to be. There are peculiarities to be considered, disagreements to be met, adjustments to be made, temperaments to be harmonized, differences to be healed, loyalties to be strengthened, shocks to be cushioned, and foundations to be built.

The husband lives in a world of action, business, and conquest. The wife lives in a world of emotions, love, devotion, and maternity. The husband tends to be materialistic and objective; the wife is intuitive and subjective. Before marriage, they were bound together in an indissoluble unity. Now there is diversity. Instead of one world, they now face two worlds.

If their love is to endure, it must be based on something higher than themselves. Something bigger than either one must be central. Happiness does not come with marriage. It has to be cultivated and earned through continual adjustment, through the development of mutual understanding, and through compromise. Count Keyserling says, "Marriage is not by nature a condition of happiness." Since marriage is made up of two imperfect individuals, he believes that necessarily it "involves conflict or tension of adjustment between two lives which are seeking to be one."

This implies that married couples will find occasions for argument, conflict, disagreement, and dispute. Indeed, married life would be rather dull and colorless without them. The important thing is not that there are issues but that issues be adjusted quickly and leave no scars. They should never be allowed to accumulate and gather resentment. Agitations, irritations, and jealousies that are allowed to smoulder make psychological dynamite, and dynamite has a way of blowing up at the wrong time. Procrastination in this case is dangerous. The battle and argument may be necessary, but it should be settled before bedtime. It is a good rule to dispose of differences on the spot. The great lubricants in marital difficulties are forgiveness, tolerance, sympathy, and love.

It is a tragic thing for a husband to transfer his affection from wife to another woman, or for a wife to transfer her allegiance to another man than her husband. Yet it happens every day.

The wife gives the best years of her life to her husband, gives love, devotion, and honest service, and then finds to her consternation that he is giving to another love that rightly belongs to her.

What should a wife do in a situation of this kind? Well, the first thing she must do is to set her husband free; that is, she must give him his freedom in her thought. Does she do it? Very seldom. She hangs on to him for dear life. What is hers is hers, and she is not going to share it. She fights and hangs on; the more she fights, the more determined he is to be free. An emotional tug of war develops with the wife on the losing end. But if she had set her husband free in God, if she had taken him back to the Fountain of all Love within her own soul and said, "Lord, let this, my love, be purified and lifted up and made one with Thy Love," the threatened marriage would have emerged unharmed.

Whenever the problem come to mind of the wife, she should think of her husband as a soul that is searching for itself. She should see him as strong, noble, pure steadfast, and true.

She should realize that the affinity between them can never be sullied or weakened by any outside force. The grieving or mistreated husband, in turn, must follow the pattern of release in order to hold his wife.

Dr. Norman Peale* tells of a woman who told him that she was getting very suspicious of her husband. She said she had every reason to believe that her husband was interested in another woman. "At first," he said, "I did not take much stock in her assertions, but she finally proved to me that what she said was so."

"I assured her that she could get him back because she had had him first. 'Nobody can take him away from you,' I said. 'unless you let him go. You are his first love; he has an affinity for you that he does not have for anybody else. You are his wife. Also, you have legality and decency on your side. The other woman has nothing on her side except a passing glamour. And you can surpass that glamour and get him back.' 'How can I do it?' she asked.

I did not know at the time or I would have quoted Marlene Dietrich. Someone asked her to become a glamourous person. 'The secret to glamour,' she said, 'is plenty of soap and water and an untroubled mind.'

At any rate I told this woman what I thought she might do, though my suggestion had nothing about cosmetics or soap and water in it: I throw that in for what it is worth.

One day she called me. 'My husband has an engagement to take this woman out to dinner tonight. We are defeated. It is all over. I can't fight any longer.

---

* Used by permission to the author.

'I will tell you what to do. Find out wh
dinner and go there yourself. Walk right

'Oh, I couldn't create a scene,' she proteste<

'I don't mean that you are to go there physica.
'Send your mind there.' And I told her about        ˻nic
powers of the human mind; how by faith she coˌˌˌu send her
mind out into space.

'Visualize him at the dinner table. Surround him with
loving thoughts, with faith thoughts. Think about him as a
fine person he really is. Affirm that he will not continue on
his present course. All evening pray and send out faith and
loving thoughts to him.'

'I don't feel very loving,' she protested. 'I'm too mad.' But I
insisted, and finally she agreed.

What do you think happened? At ten o'clock, he walked in.

'Did you have a good time?' she asked him.

'I was never so bored in my life,' he said.

Does this sound foolish? He cured him; we stopped his
wandering. And today you never saw a more completely
devoted and loving husband. Faith. It is a tremendous force,
a powerful factor. Put your faith in God, in His presence, in
His guidance. Put your faith in faith. The simpler you can be
in taking faith and using it, the better results you will get."

In the morning mail is a letter from a woman whose problem
is a jealous husband. Another wife tells of a drinking husband.
Both men, according to their wives, are making life unbearable.

ifficult to handle such problems by mail. The
ant thing to realize in this kind of difficulty is that no
se is hopeless. In spite of all appearances to the contrary,
there is a way out. The Army Engineer Corps has a motto
that every married couple should have in the home: "The
difficult we do immediately: the impossible it takes a little
longer." That is a concise statement of the metaphysical
principle of demonstration. God opens a way where there
is no way. *"The things which are impossible with men are
possible with God."* Think defeat, and defeat will come. Think
frustration, and you will be frustrated. Think victory, and
you will be victorious.

Divorce is not the answer to the challenges of marriage
that prove difficult to meet. It is very easy for one to throw
up his hands and run to a lawyer. But the solution comes
through facing the real cause of estrangement. That trouble
is not in the situation that has arisen but within one or
both of the parties to a marriage. If one person corrects the
fault within himself, the fault in the other person cannot
continue to exist. It takes two to make quarrel, but it takes
only one to avoid it.

"But things look bad," you say. "and there is no hope of a
reconciliation." Then you are denying the love of God. You are
assuming that there was never any real love between you. Have
you gone within and tackled this problem in your own mind and
heart? Have you loosed the erring member of your family and
given him freedom in your thought? Probably not. You still feel
that your guidance, wisdom, and direction are indispensable.
The whole difficulty is likely to be that one member is chafing
under the restraint of the possessive love of the other whose
selfishness keeps him from realizing what he is doing.

There are three steps that must be taken by those seeking a way out of the distress of marital difficulties.

## STEP 1. FACE YOUR RESPONSIBILITY.

Did it every occur to you that all this trouble may have come about through your own negative attitudes—jealousy, selfishness, and greed? Why not put every member of the family on his own and let him develop in his own way? Genuine love gives and, by virtue of giving, draws to itself love in return. Facing your own responsibility is the first step toward breaking the bottleneck of marital difficulty.

## STEP 2. CHANGE YOUR REACTIONS.

Drop all thought of divorce or separation and purge yourself of all jealousy, personality, and selfishness. Drive out all thoughts of criticism, condemnation, injury, and injustice. See your loved one as God made him—perfect. Jesus said in many ways, "Love your offending partner." Love all the faults right out of him. Dissolve all bitter and antagonistic thoughts in your consciousness by your love. Let it fill your whole world. Let it encompass everyone within it.

Spiritual Law is definite. If you have grievances, do more than talk about them. Change the attitude of mind that is giving power to them. The offending mate is not the cause of the trouble; your reaction to the offense is the real culprit.

Erring husbands and wives are but the embodiment of confused ideas. If one of the two involved changes his consciousness, he changes the condition. In order to help the offending party, he must first establish the consciousness of love and harmony in his mind. He must eliminate all antipathy, antagonism, fretfulness, irritability, and confusion. He must bring God into the situation by recognizing Him as the only Presence and Power. The offender could not disrupt the relationship unless his offense was accepted as a personal belief.

When anger is expressed, the peace-maker knows that because God is all, anger has no power to hurt him and no power to affect the person in whom it originates. He meets animosity by dissolving it in Divine Love. He realizes that Divine Wisdom reveals his right place in the scheme of things and expresses harmoniously through him. He remains peaceful and recognizes only the Divine. His acceptance of this Truth heals the breach.

## STEP 3. TREAT FOR HARMONY.

*"Pray for them,"* said Jesus. Prayer is the great method of the reconciling estranged persons — of dissolving discordant elements. It is love in action.

The word of the worker operating through the one Mind present in all dissolves every appearance of hurt, all though of strife, and all belief is separation. This process of purification eliminates friction and misunderstanding and adjusts and harmonizes irritating, opposing, and selfish interests. does your mate jar you and annoy you? Then practice the Presence of God as Love. Put love to work in every thought, word, and deed. In love, there is no loss. What we are related to in Consciousness we can never lose.

Jesus did not see people for what they seemed to be but for what they really were. His method was to look beyond the appearance of discord and confusion to the Reality behind. *"Be ye therefore perfect, even as your Father which is in Heaven is perfect."* See your loved one as he is in God. Hold the image of perfection for him. The mental image that you hold is creative. As you hold a perfect image of another, you not only emulate God but he becomes a co-creator with Him. Do you see how this law works in family relationships? When you bring Him into the situation, the marital rift is mended.

"But," says one, "Joan is so and so, and thus and such!" "Why, John is so full of deceit and lust and temper that there is no room for anything good. How could I possibly see him as perfect?" inquires another.

You can't see the perfect man unless you look past the physical man to the Christ within him. Are you without sin and short-comings yourself? Then why do you presume to cast stones at Joan or at John? No imperfection has power unless it is accepted as your own belief. *"He that is without sin among you, let him cast the first stone."*

Did you every try blessing John, or Mary, or Bill? Blessing has a very salutary effect, you know. Bless each member of your family whenever he comes to your thought. Speak the word *Love* through your home many times a day. Maybe your marriage is on the rocks, but it doesn't have to stay here. Bless your marriage with mental image of perfection. Bless the conditions, thoughts, words, and deeds that have brought your marital relations to such a frightful pass. Bless the problems that you seemingly are unable to meet. When there is fretful, irritable, or confused person in the home, apply the Principle of Love. God knows how to break any deadlock between husband and wife, but He has to have a clear channel to work through. Will you e such a channel? Then start today. Live in the love of God, and carry the mental image of perfection wherever you go. Say:

GOD'S LOVE IS IN ME. GOD'S LOVE RADIATES THROUGH ME. NO ONE CAN ESCAPE IT. IT SUSTAINS, SOOTHES, AND PROTECTS EVERY MEMBER OF MY FAMILY: YOU, _____, AND YOU _____. GOD'S LOVE GUIDES ME, STRENGTHENS ME, BLESS ME, AND THROUGH ME BLESSES THE WHOLE WORLD. FROM NOW ON, I SHALL SEE ONLY THE GOOD. I SHALL FORGET MYSELF AND BECOME AN IMITATOR OF GOD.

LOVE WARMS ME WITH ITS SPIRIT OF FORGIVENESS. MY HEART IS WARM WITH LOVE TOWARD EVERYBODY AND EVERYTHING. MY MIND, MY LIFE, MY AFFAIRS, AND MY WHOLE WORLD ARE TRANSFORMED BY LOVE.

I PUT MY FAITH IN HIS PRESENCE AND POWER. FATHER, I THANK THEE THAT THOU HAST BROKEN THROUGH THE RESISTANCE IN MY CONSCIOUSNESS. IN THE BOUNDLESS CIRCLE OF THY LOVE, THY GLORIOUS WILL IS DONE.

If you followed the suggestion that you try to write something that would be helpful to Helen and Jerry and to Jim and Margaret, get your paper and now reread it. Has your understanding of the way to meet a marital problem increased through your effort to put the solution in words and through your reading? Has our understanding helped you in your own relationships?

## DO'S AND DON'TS FOR MARRIED COUPLES

1. Always be true to each other—true in act, word, and thought, Lies always catch up with you; nothing destroys confidence so quickly.

2. Be completely loyal to each other. Disloyalty is a wound that never heals. Love may continue, but it may never be the same again.

3. Pray every day for an understanding heart. It is one of the most vital and indispensable things in married life. Pray together about your mutual problems. Joint prayer is one of the great cohesive forces of married life.

4. Insist upon having your own home even if it is inadequate for your needs. Living with in-laws is not economy. No house is big enough for two families.

5. Do not allow liquor in your home. Alcohol produces nothing but misery. Many divorces stem from cocktail parties. When the controls are down, almost anything can happen. Jealousy engendered on such an occasion often takes over and end in divorce.

6. Live within your income. Do not buy on credit. Debts involved in keeping up with the people next door led to many a divorce court. Buy only what you can pay for.

7. Make a deliberate effort to have the conversation at the table interesting and amusing. Store up things to tell at this time. Never discuss sickness or other negatives.

8. Forget old love affairs after marriage. *"Forsaking all others"* means to forget old flames. Do not try to make your mate jealous by pretending to be interested in a third party.

9. Keep your courtship alive to the end of your days. Recall the many thoughts things you did for each other when you were courting and keep on doing them. Be interested in each other and in each other's interests. Participate in as many things as you can together. Make yourselves attractive to each other. Keep appearances up. Do not become careless in dress. Refinement and modestly always pays off.

10. Acquaint yourself with the more intimate side of marriage by reading such books as these:

Foster, R. G. *Marriage and Family Relationship.*Popenoe, Paul. *Marriage Is What You Make It.*Mudd, Emily. *The Practice of Marriage Counseling.*

11. Get into the habit of going to church on Sunday and take the whole family with you. Give some time to spiritual reading and prayer every day – preferably at breakfast, at dinner, and before going to bed.

12. Keep your expectancy level high but take nothing for granted. Work at the job of establishing success in marriage.

13. Avoid making comparisons. Your married an individual with assets and liabilities in emotions, habits, and character. The day for comparison is over.

14. Present a solid front before your children Children can sense lack of unity when they feel that father and mother disagree. Both parents lose in such a case. If a mistake is

judgment has been made by one, discuss it in private but never in front of the children.

15. Wives — Get the housework, particularly the laundry, out of the way before your husband gets home in the evening. There is nothing that will magnify the tiredness of a tired mind so quickly as unmade beds, dirty dishes, and an unkempt home.

16. Husbands — Leave your business at the store or office. Lock up your problems in the desk or safe. Work conscientiously during the working hours. Then make as efficient use of the other sixteen hours of the day. Home and family are entitled to their share of your time and attention.

Robert A. Russell

# Chapter VIII.    In Spite Of . . .
# The Threat of Divorce

My years of experience at the SHRINE OF THE HEALING PRESENCE in trying to help those in the throes of marital difficulties have convinced me that most disrupted marriages can be salvaged by the application of a few simple principles. These principles have been tested and proved in the laboratory of experience. They work for the married couples who practice hem.

## 1. MAKE A PLACE FOR RELIGION IN YOUR LIVES.

The first and more basic principle in happy and enduring marriage, according to a writer for the Church World Press, is a "common allegiance to Christ and His Church, a family devotion to God and the doing of His Will — these qualities bind the family into oneness, increase and magnify joys, sustain in times of difficulties, and fill the home with untold blessings."

It makes no difference what the religion may be. Put it to work in the home. Husband and wife should go to church together and pray together. They should return thanks at meals, have morning and evening prayer, and hold periods of Silence to listen to God's Guidance. When problems come, they should seek the answer in united prayer.

They will soon learn that trusting God for everything will smooth the path on which they walk as nothing else will. Trusting Him will not only make the crooked places straight, but will strengthen the original loyalty on which the marriage was based.

## 2. Work to Understand Your Mate.

Solidarity in marriage is not a matter of salary, furniture house or children, but of mutual understanding. If you go into it expecting too much, you will be disappointed. Marriage like anything else is what you make it. You will take out of it exactly what you put into it and nothing more.

You must not only understand the nature of marriage but also the nature of your mate. You must have perspective, sympathetic devotion, and understanding. If there are essential differences between you, you must make allowances for them. Marriage is a matter of give and take.

## 3. Cultivate a Sense of Humor.

Would you keep your marriage happy? Then cultivate a sense of humor. Don't take yourself too seriously. Most marital woes come from disregard of this fundamental rule. We exaggerate unimportant things, our little selves included. We get the cart before the horse. The result is conflict, division, and confusion. Are you egotistic, bombastic, caustic, and bad tempered? Then you are taking yourself too seriously. You are out of balance. You are overestimating your importance. Why are you trying to keep this little ego alive? Why are you so cramped and uncompromising? Is it that you want to be superior? That you are afraid that you will be unappreciated? Why do you carry that chip around on your shoulder? Why do you strain at gnats and swallow camels? Why do you clamor for recognition? Isn't it because you are putting last things first? Are you trying to be God? Why don't you whittle yourself down to size? Why don't you learn to laugh at yourself? To laugh at calamities? It is much easier to laugh your mate out of his rancor than it is to argue or scold him out of it. If you must be serious about important things. Let go, my friend, and forget yourself. If you have trouble with others, say this prayer: "God keep me from taking myself too seriously."

### 4. LEARN TO EXPRESS APPRECIATION FREELY.

Married couples tend to take too much for granted. Let me write that indelibly in you minds. One of the deepest needs of human nature is the desire to be appreciated. Everyone craves appreciation. No marriage can stand up without it. Everything responds to praise; without it, life grows mediocre, colorless, ordinary, and dull.

If your husband has put over a big deal, tell him how proud you are. Show him your appreciation. It will not only warm his hear for the moment, but it will spur him on to greater achievement. Praise him for everything that merits praise; be silent about things that need censure. Talk the unpleasant things over when you are both calm and relaxed.

Was the dinner good, Mr. Husband? Then praise it. Show your appreciation. Does our wife have a new dress? Then make over it. Tell her how pretty she looks. Practice seeing the things that are good and magnifying them.

A young girl sent this question to a newspaper: "What must I do to win and hold a man?" The reply came back: "Learn 400 ways of saying, 'I think you are wonderful.'"

## 5. Build a Home, Not Merely a House.

A Christian home is built not only of material bricks, stucco, nails, lumber, and metal, but of such intangibles as harmony, peace, love, and patience. Its value is determined not by the drapes and furniture not by the color scheme but by the attitudes, feelings, and thoughts those who dwell within it.

If the atmosphere of your home is one of contention and strife, you can help to change these conditions. You can be a peacemaker. You can radiate love and harmony. You can bless the members of your household with the thought: "There is but One Presence and Power in this home — God, the Good, the Omnipotent." If there is quarreling or fault - finding, you can help to overcome it by being peaceful and harmonious yourself. If there is resignation or despair, you can help to meet it by being light-hearted and free. Even one person holding the Truth can change the whole atmosphere of the home.

## 6. Preserve a Sense of Proportion.

There are a lot of married couples who need the rebuke that Jesus gave to the religious leaders of His day. *"You blind guides! straining out that gnat while you gulp down the camel!"* *"You Pharisees,"* He said, *"are very scrupulous. If a gnat gets into your wine, you strain it out with the utmost care. But f a camel gets in, you gulp him down, hair, humps, hoofs, and all."* What is Jesus rebuking in this statement? The making mountains out of mole hills, the straining over trifle, the magnifying little things. This habit is one of he besetting of people who come to me for personal counseling, about sixty per cent come about marital difficulties — family feuds, disputes, and misunderstandings.

Husbands are estranged from their wives, and wives are estranged from their husbands. It is not the big problem that disrupts the home life of these persons; accumulated petty, small, insignificant things are responsible. Big problems draw the partners in marriage closer together. Little problems send them to Reno.

There is only one cure for this unfortunate habit; there is only one way to keep things in their right proportion. That one way is to practice the Presence of God—to put him at the center of our lives.

We must discipline mind and tongue. We must lift Christ up in our consciousness. We must think big thoughts— magnanimous thoughts. We must allow nothing to e expressed through us except that which contributes to the greater good. If we think little thoughts, we become little. If we magnify the little things in the home, we miss the big things. If we think big thoughts, we become big.

## 7. Practice Surrendering the Self.

Back of every failure in marriage is the failure to surrender the self. Until husbands and wives get themselves out of the center (which belongs to God), they will continue to be a problem to one another. In the parlance of the street, they will get in one another's hair. Self-centeredness is self-destructive. It reverses the Law that says, *"He that loseth his life* [surrenders the self] *shall find it."* It is my conviction, after years of observation, that there is nothing the destroys connubial felicity so quickly as egocentricity. When husband or wife tries to hold the center, or worse still when both try, marriage ends in frustration. It is obvious that a husband and wife must establish—an area of understanding—a region of mutual trust—a recognition of the third Partner in the important business of making success of marriage.

Selfishness is a disease; its only reward is unhappiness. To be bounded on four sides by self is hell not only for the individual but also for the other members of his household. Standing at the center, he finds that nothing comes out right. When he gets himself out of the center, problems fall into their places along with the solutions that come into being simultaneously with the problems and that only await his recognition.

Since man is made to love and worship something bigger than himself, the first step to happiness and success is to give himself to God. Taking this step changes the whole trend of your life. You are no longer a self-conscious person; you become a God-conscious person. Having shifted the gravity of your thought from self to God, you see that, *"old things are passed away"* and *"all things become new."* You become relaxed and free. You no longer get in the way of others because God has His way in you.

Do you see how important self-righteousness is? If a husband and wife life only for each other, they "will become so possessive and jealous of each other that they will destroy their love by selfishness," writes John Homer Miller.* He retells a pertinent story that the psychologist, William James, once told in a lecture on Motherhood.

A teacher asked a boy this question in fractions: "Suppose your mother baked an apple pie and there were seven of you, your parents and five children, what part of the pie would be your portion?"

---

* Miller, John Henry. *Take a Look at Yourself.* Abingdon-Cokesbury Press.

"A sixth," answered the boy.

"But there are seven of you," said the teacher. "Don't you know anything about fractions?"

"Yes," replied the boy "I know about fractions, but I know about mothers, too. Mother would say she didn't want any pie.

Then Miller adds this pertinent comment: "Success in marriage depends upon a husband a wife's each giving up his piece of pie for the other and both giving it up for something greater than themselves."

What is this tremendous force that draws a man and woman together in the bods of Holy Matrimony? Love. What is Love? There is only one answer — *"God is love."* Love is the greatest force in the world. It beautifies and enriches whatever it touches. It is all of God's attributes in one. Too many people today think of love in terms of sensual pleasure. They identify it with the animal instincts for that is the only love they know. Sensual love is sentimental, selfish, and immature. It has no depth or permanence.

What do you mean when you say "I love you"? Do you mean the same thing as when you say, "I love a grapefruit," or "I love cantaloupe"? If the grapefruit could speak, it would ask you what you mean by the statement, "I love grapefruit." It might say, "What kind of love is it that squeezes the best out of me and then throws me away?" What do you mean when you say, "I love my boy." "I love my wife," "I love my friend"? Do you mean what the word implies or do you mean *I want to possess you? I want to gratify myself?*

Perhaps the marriage office for the Church should be changed. "Do you take this man for your lawful wedded husband?" and "Do you take this woman for your lawful wedded wife?"

might read "Do you give yourself, body, soul, and spirit to this man?" and "Do you give yourself body, soul and spirit to this woman?" That change would put the emphasis where it belongs, wouldn't it?

## 8. Know That Your Love is One With Divine Love.

Couples may get along for a time, with the love established on the basis of the sensual side of their natures, but such love does not last. When the freshness of physical charms has gone sensual love dies. When a woman tries to hold her husband by keeping his animal passions alive, the marriage is likely to be of short duration. Genuine love is characterized by refinement, devotion, kindness, nobility, spirituality, generosity, patience, and self sacrifice. It goes beyond the physical to the Eternal.

Love is the greatest force in the world. Love sees only the good. It does not argue, censure, or divide. Seeing only the good, it throws the mantle of forgiveness over the faults of others. It takes the weak and makes them strong. It takes the sick and makes them well. It takes the divided and makes them one.

## 9. Be Patient.

*"Love beareth all things, endureth all things."*

Do you say, "I love my husband," and yet have no patience with him? Do you go into a violent tirade over the aim that missed or the blunder that seems to you stupid? Then your love is weak. You are intolerant. Perhaps you need to learn that in a true marriage there is no *I*, or *he*, or *she* but just *we*; no *me*, or *him*, or *her* but just *us*; no *mine* or *yours*, no *his* or *hers*, but just *ours*.

The impatient person tries to work things out in his own strength. He does not take Christ into his affairs. When he meets with frustration, his impatience increases, but when he turns to the Power within him, he develops patience. He finds that he becomes patient in the situation in which he gives himself and all his affairs into God's keeping.

There are may things that make for confusion and unhappiness in a home, but if patience is lacking, the family falls apart. Patience comes through understanding that God is an instant and unfailing help.

## 10. Use the Strength That Love Gives You.

True love is strong enough to meet every human need. It does not change with every wind that blows It is the same yesterday, today, and forever. To practice love in the home is to have heaven on earth. Weak love will fail us in the hour of need; strong love will see us through.

Such a love does not wax and wane. It is not based on personality. When love is based on the understanding, there is no difficulty between husband and wives. It doesn't make any difference whether the problem is domestic, financial, or personal, the surest help in meeting it is an enduring love.

## 11. DON'T BE AFRAID TO BE COMPASSIONATE.

Perhaps no aspect of love is so much needed in human life today as compassion and tenderness. A person without compassion is a sentence isolated from the Book of Life. He is cold, unfeeling, and uncertain. If peace and happiness are to reign in the home, love must have full sway. Husbands and wives must learn to express themselves in praise, in endearing phrases, in approval and approbation.

Although Peter denied our Lord three times, Jesus was most tender to His attitude toward him. When the cock crew, Peter expected a rebuke from Jesus; instead He gave him a look of tenderness that pierced the disciple's heart like a rapier thrust. On the Resurrection Morn, Mary came running to the disciples with the message: "The Master has risen, and He told me to go tell His disciples—and Peter." A special message for Peter! Think how it must have lifted his heavy heart. John arrived at the sepulchre first but did not go in. Peter rushed in. He was ashamed and wanted forgiveness; he wanted to make things right with Jesus. But Jesus was not there.

Here then is a drama of Divine Love. *"And Jesus, when He came out, saw much people, and was moved with compassion toward them."* No matter what provocation or injustice we face, we must practice the tenderness and compassion of Christ. The Father forgave the Prodigal Son without condemnation. *"Pray for them which despitefully use you, and persecute you."* Divine Love is immutable. A family dispute or controversy will sometimes break up a home based on human love. A little misunderstanding will separate friends. Personal differences will stir up anger. But you have no more right to stay mad twenty-four hours than you have to set fire to your neighbor's house or throw red pepper into his eyes. If genuine love were present, it would not change. God's Love is unchangeable.

## 12. Don't Take Love For Granted.

Many of us are unable to evaluate our blessings until they are gone. Who realizes the value of eyesight until it is gone? Who realizes the value of health until it is gone? Who realizes the value of loved ones until they are gone?

We must not take love for granted. When love is dead, it is the deadest thing in the world. Many husbands and wives have discovered that sad fact too late. It is much easier to keep love alive than it is to resurrect it when it is dead. In fact, resurrections of love are very rare. Magnify love, and it will become the greatest power in your life. Neglect it, and it will wither and die. *"God so loved the world that He gave His only begotten Son that whosoever believeth on Him should not perish, but have everlasting life."* Here is the Universe in miniature. Love is self-givingness. No sacrifice is too great for it to make. It is glorious, transforming, and uplifting. Someone has well said, "To love abundantly is to live abundantly. To love forever is to live forever. To have love is to have God, and to have God is to have all."

# A PRAYER FOR A MARRIED COUPLE

O God, our Heavenly Father, who hast consecrated the state of Matrimony, let Thy richest blessings rest upon us and upon our home. Increase and beautify our love for each other day by day; pour into our hearts such patience, wisdom, and understanding that we may see and speak only the good. So deepen our consciousness of Thy Presence that we may be quick to forgive and immune to hurt.

Help us to realize that we are surrounded by an atmosphere of Love and that we are guided and governed by the impulse of love. Where there is confusion, establish peace. Where there is suspicion, establish confidence. Where there is fear, establish faith. Where there is error, establish Truth. Where there is jealousy, establish trust. Make us living temples of Thy Truth, strong in body, sound in mind, loving in heart, devout in Spirit. And grant, O Lord, that we may bring out each other's best, through Jesus Christ our Lord. Amen.

# Chapter IX.  In Spite Of . . .
# The Responsibilities of Parenthood

*"Let the man of God . . . come again and teach us what we shall do unto the child,"* said Manoah, the father of Samson, three thousand years ago.

When Solomon was given the opportunity of choosing what he wanted more than anything else in the world, he chose understanding in order that he might be a wise and successful ruler of his people. God was so pleased with his request that He promised him in addition honor, long life, and riches.

There is such an urgency about the child problem today that parents might well profit by Solomon's example and ask for wisdom and understanding in training their children in the way they should go. As most parents will agree, the problem is becoming more and more difficult with the increased complexity of our living and the great differences in the lives of succeeding generations.

We hear and reach much about juvenile delinquency in these days, and statistics prove that there is a basis for our concern. Over fourteen per cent of arrests in 1951 were of individuals under twenty-one years of age. Those under twenty-five years make up twenty-nine per cent of the total arrests in the United States and its possessions. Crimes within this group were serious, and the proportion is startling. While this segment of the population (persons under twenty-five) comprised only 28.9% of total number arrested, 52.9% of the total arrests for robbery, 60.3% for burglary, 43.9% for larceny, and 68.4% for automobile thefts were within this group.

The number of arrests of persons of all ages, recorded and finger printed by the Federal Bureau of Investigation, increases steadily (1949-792,029, 1950-793,671, 1951-831,288). But the percentage of arrests for juveniles (those eighteen and under) increases, too, 1949 (showing 7.5%, 1950-7.7% and 1951-7.95.[*]

Diogenes, a Greek philosopher who lived three centuries before the Christian era, is said to have "struck the father when the son swore."[†]

The phrase, *juvenile delinquency*, shifts the blame from the parent to the child, but in the final analysis, there is no delinquency but parental delinquency.

Try to explain it as you will, our moral fiber seems to show signs of breaking down today.

We have improved our living, but weakened our manhood. We have push buttons, gadgets, inventions, and appliances for almost everything required in keeping house, but we have deadened the moral sense of our womanhood. In the world of business, we have the telephone, the telegraph, television, computing machines, intercommunication systems, and unbelievably rapid transportation, but slow motion in the direction of increased spiritual awareness and understanding prevails.

---

[*] All data are taken from *Uniform Crime Reports,* issued by the United State Department of Justice.
[†] Robert Burton in *Anatomy of Melancholy.*

What good is quantity if it lessens quality? What good is highly refined and adulterated food if it impairs our digestion? What good is speed if it increases disaster? What good is fun if it dims our vision? What good is freedom if it breaks down morality?

We lament the simple and restricted lives of our forebears, but we forget the blessings and virtues that their type of living produced. They, as a rule, had healthy resilient bodies, strong clear minds, unassailable convictions, and a firm grip upon the realities of life.

The contrast on the moral plane is odious. Last year there were 390,000 divorces in this country alone, to say nothing of the countless thousands of desertions and separations. The divorce rate has steadily increased since 1940. At that time two out of every thousand marriages ended in divorce. During the years in which armed forces overseas were included in the figures (1946-1946), the rate rose to 3.5 and 4.3 respectively. Excluding the armed forces overseas, it was 3.4 in 1947, 2.8 in 1948, 2.6 in 1949.*

Newspapers and magazines give a great deal of space to the discussion of the problems of the home in which one parent has defaulted and to the responsibility of society in such cases. Legislation is becoming more and more stringent in setting up penalties for this evasion of responsibility.

Barbara Heggie writing in Good Housekeeping, October, 1951, under the title "Runaway Husbands," says that in the eight years preceding 1950, there was an increase of 42% in the number of men who walked out on their wives and children.

---

* Figures are from *Statistical Abstract of the United States,* published by the Department of Justice.

She adds, "Currently, there are fourteen runaway husbands for every runaway wife."

"More than a hundred thousand husbands run away from their families in this country every year," said Clarence Woodbury in Woman's Home Companion for September, 1949. Is there anything surprising about the number of juvenile delinquents when there are a "million abandoned dependents in the United States, 750,000 of whom are children under sixteen"?

To succeed as a parent today is a costly thing, but it is much more costly to fail. "Why should I have any great love for my mother?" asked a young woman the other day. "She never had any for me. When I was very young, I was given over to nurses and governesses while my mother lived gaily in Paris and London. She was always on the go and always too busy to give me any attention. She gave all her time to society and knew practically nothing of me or of my welfare." The indifference of a child is a fearful price for a parent to pay, but it is the logical price of neglect—of the failure of a parent to live up to his responsibilities and obligations.

When I heard this daughter's indictment of her mother, my mind wandered back to the prophet's rebuke of mothers in Lamentations. *"The daughter of my people is become cruel like the ostriches in the wilderness."* The ostrich of that day was held with great disdain and scorn. Job said, *"The ostrich leaveth her eggs in the earth, and warmeth them in the dust, and forgetteth that the foot may crush them, or that the wild beast may break them. She is hardened against her young ones, as though they were not hers."*

Why was the prophet so stirred up? What was he disturbed about? Was it a drunken father beating his son that filled him with indignation? No. It was the action of the mothers of that day. Why? Why all this tirade against the mothers? Were they blowing cigarette smoke into the sensitive eyes of their infants? Were they refusing them food, clothing, and shelter? Were they leaving them unattended? No. They were guilty only of the cruelty of forgetfulness and neglect.

If the Prophet Job had been speaking to the mother of today, he might have said, "She is so busy with social activities, permanent waves, lectures, movies, cards, clubs, and child welfare agencies that she hasn't time to look after her own children."

"But to compare a mother to an ostrich—this sounds more than a little exaggerated," you say. "Why should Job go to such extremes in this thing?" For the simple reason that mothers were not putting first things first. They were not recognizing the importance of the child; they had no concept of their duty to him. They did not seem to understand that the child who is neglected is headed for disaster. They were not preparing their children for maturity. They were not providing the wholesome homes and the family security that every child needs. Do you know where most problem children come from? They come from neglected homes—not necessarily homes in which poverty is a factor. The "poor little rich girl" is not an impossibility. Without love, and care, and active interest, a child fails to develop a sense of security. He may tend to become rebellious and demand attention in unpleasant, unconstructive ways, or he may withdraw from the situation in his sense of isolation. When a child cannot find a place in his home and family group that is satisfying, he acquires strange and disagreeable characteristics and attitudes.

Parenthood places an enormous obligation and responsibility upon the father and mother. Of course, this same obligation and responsibility can be and is for countless parents their greatest joy. The full realization of the uniqueness of the parent-child relationship will motivate action of the highest type. Food and shelter can be supplied by others, but no one but parents can give the child parental love. No one else can give the same training. "The mother's heart is the child's schoolroom," wrote Henry Ward Beecher, and George Herbert said, "One father is more than a hundred school-masters."

"But aren't you overemphasizing the need?" asks he complacent parent. Not at all. There is probably more spiritual neglect of children today than ever before. Would you wilfully neglect the physical needs of your child? No, because you know he would soon die if you did. Neglect of his body spells visible disaster. The quickest way to kill a baby is to let him alone. Then why neglect the mental and spiritual hungers that are even more important than physical hunger? Your child is a three-fold being—body, soul, and spirit. He needs mental and spiritual food as well as material food.

Now listen to the prophet again: *"The tongue of the nursing child cleaveth to the roof of his mouth for thirst."* The prophet was saying that children have needs that cannot be met by milk and bread alone. Every parent should be required to read "The Childrens' Charter," which was drawn up in Washington in 1930. Point One says that every child must have "Spiritual and moral training to help him stand firm under the pressure of life."

Ah! There's the rub! Here is the place in which so many millions of American parents fall down. For church and church school, we have substituted the automobile and the picture show. For grace at the table, we have substituted radio and television. Do you wonder why paganism is so rampant among us? It is not that parents today are essentially atheistic but that they act like atheists.

A juvenile judge made the statement not long ago that of some four thousand boys under twenty-one whom he had sentenced, only three had been active in church school. How long is it going to take parents to realize that criminals are made by parental neglect?

Indifference to children is a grave sin. Mothers spend hours learning how to make drapes, hats, dresses, and tasty dishes but spend practically no time in learning how to prepare children for maturity. They give untiring effort in securing efficient teachers of the dance and of music for the child and little time and effort in seeing that he has an opportunity to learn to thin and to pray. They devote many afternoons learning how to play bridge and canasta, and no time to learning how to make a Christian home. I assure you that strong, useful, and responsible children don't just happen. Someone has to work and pray night and day to achieve this result.

Job berated the mothers, too, for their lack of vision. They failed to realize the rich rewards of faithfulness to their task.

Abraham Lincoln said, "All I am or can be I owe to my angel mother."

Lew Wallace, the author of *Ben Hur*, said, "God could not be everywhere, so He made mothers."

Susanna Wesley, the mother of John Wesley who founded Methodism, wrote: "What shall I render the Lord for all His mercies? I intend to be more particularly careful with the soul of this child that Thou has so mercifully provided for than I have ever been; that I may instill into his mind the principles of true religion and virtue."

The Bible reads like a Hall of Fame for great mothers. There is Elizabeth, the mother of John, Hannah the mother of Samuel, devoted Eunice with little Timothy at her knee. Towering above them all is the Maid of Nazareth, the Mother of Jesus. Yes, my friend, Motherhood is a costly thing, but its rewards are great.

Fathers are parents too, although one does not always think of the father in connection with character moulding. In most families, father does not take much responsibility in this area. Father himself is largely responsible for this most unfortunate attitude. He is so busy making a living and tussling with the world that he cannot be bothered with the youngsters' upbringing. The children turn out good or bad, not because of the father but in spite of him. There are exceptional fathers, on the other hand, who are just as loving, unselfish, and devoted to their children as the mother.

Perhaps a change of attitude and feeling in the family would encourage father to do better. Just contrast the celebrations of Mother's Day and Father's Day in our churches and you will see what we are talking about. It is the difference between tears and a yawn. Again, father himself may be responsible for the absence of demonstration at this time, for he has, as a rule, a tendency to scoff at any sentimental display.

The poet Wordsworth in his appreciation of the possibilities in the father-child relationship wrote —

"Father! – to God himself
    We cannot give
A holier name."

But why are we prone to excuse neglect in a father and condemn it in a mother? Can't a father's failure be just as tragic as a mother's? We have the answer in the story of David and Absalom. David was successful in many things, but he was a failure as a father. He was a man of great courage, a good ruler of his people; he gave much of his vast wealth to the building of the Temple. David had everything that a king of his time could wish for — the respect and love of his subjects, great wealth, power, and prestige. But in spite of all this, he was a failure as a father.

Would you like to see the results of that failure? Then with David look in that pit out in the wilderness. Look at the magnificent body of David's son lying there cold in death. What now of his brilliant success! Here him. Hear his lament. *"O my son Absalom! my son, my son Absalom! would God I had died for thee, O Absalom, my son, my son!"*

Is this story remote from modern life? Not at all. It is re-enacted every day. I am thinking now of a friend who started with nothing and built up a fortune of four million dollars. He was known far and wide as a genius in his field. He had a luxurious home in the city and another in the country. He had servants, cars, tutors, and governesses for his children but his wealth became a liability instead of an asset. It turned sour and disruptive in the hands of his sons. It ruined their lives. This father had no time for his three growing boys, and they grew into parasites and spendthrifts. Two committed suicide; one met a violent death. This father was both a great success and a great failure. Like David he was too busy to preserve the father-son relationship which was both his responsibility and his privilege. He shifted his responsibility to others and lost his sons.

It would be wonderful if such mistakes could be corrected, if there were another time in which things could be made right or done all over. A man can fail in business and start all over. He can make a mistake on paper and correct it. But not so with the rearing of a child. "If I had only done *this* or *that*." "If I had only done my duty, this wouldn't have happened." "If I had only been a better father." How true! But the words have an empty ring. It is too late. *"O Absalom, my son."*

The rearing of a child begins at the cradle. The Roman Catholic priest says: "Give me a child until it is seven and I do not care who has it after that." In those first years, the roots grow deep. Those who stood around the cradle of John the Baptist asked *"What manner of child shall this be?"* This is the question, spoken or unspoken, that is in the heart of the parent as he looks upon his child.

The future of any babe depends largely upon how faithfully parents accept the challenge of the newborn. *"Is the young man Absalom safe?"* demanded David of all comers. The answer to your question as a parent will depend upon what you have built into your child's mind and soul.

No, you, along with grieving David, can't go out where your grown child has fallen and take his place. But you can start now to be a father to him and to take the responsibility of his welfare. You can start now to make him a blessing instead of a curse. If you do your part, no matter what happens you will have the consolation of knowing that you have done your best.

Middle-aged parents have a specific and unique problem, for they have a tendency to live in the past and to compare the children of today with the children of yesteryear. They like to think of their own childhood as different from that of the youth of today. In the good old days, children were seen and not heard. They were better mannered, more religious, more modest, more amenable, more courteous, and more suggestible than the children of today.

Do you really believe that? Then read the record and you will find that teen-age children were just as hard to handle in the 1800's as they are in the 1900's. It is true that the scope and nature of juvenile delinquencies may differ somewhat according to the social turmoil and period in which the adolescent lives, but the basic problem of the "hard to manage" is just the same in one period as in another. It is the relation of the adult to the problem that makes it seem different.

Do you find it hard to understand the speech, habits, customs, and conduct of girls that in another period we called "Flappers" — the lurid finger nail polish, lip stick, cigarettes, cocktails, necking, jeans, slacks, and juke boxes? Do you find it hard to understand the carelessness, belligerance, indifference, speed, defiance, and independence of boys that in another age called "Jelly Beans" and "Drug Store Cowboys"?

Charlotte Perkins Gilman amusingly sets forth this attitude of one generation to the succeeding one in "Twigs".*

'Tis an amusing thing to see
The topmost twigs on a growing tree
Look down with freshly-worded scorn
On the boughs by which they are upborne.
Below — beneath contempt — is sunk
The twigless, mid-Victorian trunk,
And as for roots . . . how could twigs know

---

* The author could not find the source of this poem.

There must be roots for twigs to grow?
"We twigs are Youth and Life!" they say.
"We are the World, we are Today!
This talk of boughs and trunk-bark rough,
This tribal myth of roots — old stuff!"
The tree minds not the little dears:
There were other twigs in previous years.

It is not unusual to hear a mother or father say, "I have been a failure as a parent." While such a statement is true in many instances, the parent should be sure that self-judgment is correct before the condemns himself too severely. A youngster who gets out of hand or falls from grace in his later teens does not necessarily indicate neglect or faulty training. I have seen children fall by the wayside although they have been brought up in the most ideal surroundings and under the most careful tutelege. Is it right for these parents to blame themselves for the blunders and shortcomings of their children? Certainly not. When parents have done everything in their power to give a child the right start and the right environment, they must *"Loose him and let him go."*

Your child came through you but he does not belong to you. The sooner you surrender him to God the better. There is no other way to bring him through the difficult and trying periods of his life. Belligerant children are usually seeking independence, and they must be shown how to get it. They must be allowed to grow up and stand on their own. Have you forgotten the days in which boys in their twenties were navigating sailing vessels on the seven seas and when girls in their late teens were having children and keeping up their own homes? Look today at our own war records and note the ages of the boys in action.

One of the great mistakes that fond parents make is their refusal to change their mental pictures of their children as they advance in years. There are some parents who simply will not allow their children to grow up. A son or daughter in his thirties may still be "My baby." It is not that parents are unaware of the changes that have taken place in the child, but that they will not accept the fact that the parent-child relationship must change accordingly. The result is that the child in the parent's thought is still dependent and immature and too often, accepting the pattern the parent provides, he remains dependent and immature in reality. It may be that the psychologist has a name for this kind of folly, but if he hasn't he should get one. *Smother* love is very prevalent.

Robert A. Russell

# Chapter X.    In Spite Of . . .
# The Fact That They Will Grow Up

When the child is small, he needs the mother's guidance, care, and protection. As he grows up, he must learn to think and act for himself. Will the mother let him? Well, there are two kinds of mothers—wise and unwise, sensible and foolish. The wise mother will release the child in gradual stages until he is able to stand on his own feet. The unwise mother on the other hand will hand on to the child until she is forced to let go. "You owe me something," she says, or implies by her behavior. "Think of all I have done for you. Think of my sacrifices and pain. You couldn't repay me for all I have done for you in a thousand years." Does that sound familiar? It is a frantic effort of the mother to hold the love and interest of the child by demand and appeal.

Is it any wonder that there are so many ungrateful children in the world? Mothers must learn that they attract and hold the love of their children not by what they say or do but by virtue of what they are. It is not by clinging to a child that a mother gets devotion, loyalty, and love but by releasing him. Instead of tying a child to her apron string, the wise mother will surrender him to God. She will trust the Christ within her for the guidance which he needs and the Christ within him for its reception. Instead of trying to do all his thinking for him and making him dependent upon her, she will teach him how to think and to work out of his problems for himself.

She will realize that her child has an innate capacity to accept spiritual truths and that she must capitalize it. Remembering the words of Jesus, *"Whosoever shall not receive the kingdom of God as a little child, he shall not enter therein,"* she will know that she has an opportunity to learn of him.

Give the child a deep consciousness of the presence of God, and you need have no further concern about him. "As the twig is bent, the tree inclines." If you set the spiritual course of your child's life before he is seven, in spite of anything that may happen along the way, he will come out right.

But religion is *caught* and not *taught.* The church and church school are only accessories to the home. It is the religious influence of parents that sticks to the child through life. Children are receptive and easily influenced by suggestion. Parents should be careful not only of the example they set for growing boys and girls but also of what they say. They should make sure that their words inspire rather than restrict. Words that belittle, condemn, depreciate, and disparage arrest the development of the child's soul. He who persists in calling his child a little devil may have to deal later with a big devil.

"No, Jerry, doesn't go to Sunday School. We're waiting until he is old enough to choose for himself," say many parents who have no religious affiliation and yet recognize the need of religion. This "waiting" period is disastrous. What chance of adjustment would the youth have who was not taught as a child to eat with some regularity, to sleep on an approximate schedule, to wear clothing, or to learn to read and to use figures?

No thoughtful parent allows his small child to select his own playthings at the expense of his safety, to choose his playground in the area in which traffic is heavy, to drive an automobile before he has ability and judgment, to attempt to swim without supervision and teaching.

In all types of learning, there is a period in which an art, a skill, a practice can be learned or acquired with the least possible effort. This is the "readiness" period. It depends upon such factors as age, physical development, mental capacity, experience, and environment. Primary teachers know that the degrees of "reading readiness" in the children in one class vary greatly. One of the areas for which kindergarten teachers are responsible is the development and fostering of reading readiness.

But the child's period of readiness for religious training begins with birth. His confidence that his wants will be supplied, his assurance that he is loved and understood are basic to his acceptance that his needs as well as those of his parents are met by a Power that he cannot see but of which he is a part.

The little child might well say if he had the words—

> "My mother's kiss, my
> father's hand—
> These make my world.
> I understand
> Little of all I hear or see
> But Love I sense, and
> Security,
> And that there's God.
> These things I know
> Because their love has
> proved them so."

Religious training cannot be a hit-or-miss proposition. It cannot be a cut-flower affair; it must have roots—roots that center in childhood. There is no neutral period; the child cannot "wait" to learn. He is learning all the time—from his parents, from the neighbors, from his playmates. The child who sees God as a bewhiskered individual — a cross between a king and a police judge — may have a hard time to see Him as Life and Love and Truth, as Knowledge and Principle. He should not only have an opportunity to live in a home in which the presence of the Silent Partner is an accepted fact but he should attend Church School as regularly and as conscientiously as he does the school responsible for his academic learning.

Dr. Ivan H. Hagedorn in his annual Bride and Groom Service made an apt comparison.* He says:

"The Japanese have been very successful in developing dwarf trees. They keep small what otherwise might develop into veritable giants by snipping off buds, by pruning, by removing from the soil, by cutting back the roots, and by lack of fertilization. So, trees though years old may be only eighteen inches high, with tiny leaves, instead of forty feet to which they might have grown if they had been left outdoors and developed as they should have been.

"Boys and girls can be dwarfed too, especially in goodness, by somewhat the same method.

We snip off the buds of faith; we prune away their goodness; we remove them from the soil of Christian education; we cut back the roots of love, and we fail to fertilize them by not setting before their eyes wholesome examples of cleanness in thought, word, and deed. The sad result is that the boys and girls grow big in body, but their spirit is pinched and dwarfed."

---

* Hagedorn, Ivan H. "What Is a Good Home?" *Pulpit Digest*, June, 1952.

# IN THE COUNSELOR'S STUDY

Sit with me for awhile to hear the problems voiced by parents. Note please that most of the statements are phrased in terms of the parent's frustration, or anger, or grief. But, I ask you, whose problem is greater—that of the parent who may be reaping what he has sown or that of the bewildered, unhappy, insecure youth who is trying to find himself and his place in the world of today?

"Our son is so headstrong that we cannot even reason with him. He insists on marrying a girl that we do not and cannot like. She is a Roman Catholic, and we are Protestants. My husband is furious."

"Barbara is wild. I know Barbara is wild, but I just can't do anything with her. Jamie has whipped her and I have whipped her, but we just can't conquer her."

"My sixteen-year-old daughter is out of control. She stays out until two and three in the morning, and I never know where she is. I have done everything I can do to straighten her out, but the more I remonstrate with her the more rebellious and defiant she gets."

"I need help and need it desperately. My son in high school has gotten a young girl into trouble. It is a terrible shock to us because all our hopes and plans for him have been ruined.

Let us consider the problems phrase by these parents, for they are typical.

# THE CASE OF THE OBJECTIONABLE MARRIAGE.

Many estrangements result from marriages that are unacceptable to parents. But when parents view the situation impersonally, they are the first to recognize certain facts:

1. Family unity is too precious to be broken

2. The marriage is not the important thing at the moment.

3. The attitude of parents toward it is of supreme importance.

4. Values must be weighed.

Who are they to say whether a marriage is "good" or "bad"? How can they deny the action of Spiritual Guidance to the young people while claiming it for themselves? This marriage over which they agonize may be one of the marriages made "in Heaven", despite the evidence to the contrary, despite personal opinion. Only time can tell.

If parents want to prevent a disastrous marriage, they should not resist it. Resistance at a time like this widens the gap between them and their children. The better way is to bring God into the situation by praying together about it. This is a time to use emotional control. If the objectionable person is invited to the home often and for long periods of time, one of two things may happen—

1. The youths themselves may discover such basic differences that they will "fall out" of love as easily as they "fell in."

2. Parents themselves may begin to see what their child saw in the "objectionable" individual. His good qualities may have been hidden under some superficiality. Longer acquaintance may reveal him to the parents as desirable.

But if your child marries against your desire in spite of everything, resolve to make the best of it. It is your child's happiness you are seeking. You must give your blessing and try to make it as easy for your loved one as you can, knowing that the Law of Good is at work in the situation although you see *"through a glass darkly."*

The wise mother knows that her child does not belong to her except as they both belong to God. In that consciousness, nothing can come between them. Love for a mate does not diminish love for parents. Love is not lessened by expression. It is multiplied.

*"I may speak with the tongues of men*
*and of angels,*
*but if I have no love,*
*I am a noisy gong or*
*a clanging cymbal;*
*I may prophesy, fathom all*
*mysteries and secret*
*love,*
*I may have such absolute*
*faith that I can move*
*hills from their place,*
*but if I have no love,*

*I count for nothing;*

*I may distribute all I possess*

*in charity,*

*I may give up my body to be*

*burnt,*

*but if I have no love,*

*I make nothing of it."*

*Love is very patient, very kind. Love knows no jealousy; love makes no parade, gives itself no airs, is never rude, never selfish, never irritated, never resentful; love is never glad when others go wrong, love is gladdened by goodness, always slow to expose, always eager to believe the best, always hopeful, always patient. Love never disappears.*\*

There are criteria helpful in the selection of a mate. But it is true they are not of much help to the individual who is "in love." If hasty action can be delayed, if a period of waiting can be imposed, time and longer acquaintance often resolve an affair into its true proportions.

But if there is a moment of cool detached thought on the part of either of the persons who plan to marry, attempting to answer such questions as these may be a means of defining emotions and clarifying attitudes: —

SHE should ask herself —

1. Does this man measure up to my ideals for a mate, or have I had to lower my ideals to meet his?

---

\* Moffatt Translation.

2. Do I want my children to be like him?

3. What are his chief interests in life? Am I sympathetic with them? Could I learn to understand them? To take part in them?

4. What kind of disposition has he? Is he tolerant? Understanding? Fair? Friendly? Enthusiastic?

5. Does he have religious connections? Does he go to church? Does religion play an active part in his thinking and in his action?

6. Does he like his work? Is he zealous and ambitious? Does he make a good living? How many jobs has he had? Has he been trained for a trade or profession or does he run from one job to another?

7. Does he have a good personality? Does he value a good appearance and at the same time act only on principle?

8. Has he high ideals concerning sex? Does he wish a home? Children?

HE should ask himself all the questions but 6, changing the words *man, his,* and *he,* to *woman, her,* and *she.*

But number 6, too, applies all too frequently to the woman as well as to the man, for this is a day in which a heavy percentage of husbands and wives are both wage-earners.

Ideally, this battery of questions (Number 6) should be concerned with a woman's interest in home and making her capacity for that phase of married life. Has she been trained for marriage? Does home-making appeal to her? Does it have value? Is she interested in children? Does she have a proper respect for motherhood? Does she realize that much of the success of the marriage will depend upon her ability to make the adjustment to the new life easy for her husband as well as for herself? Does she accept marriage as a partnership in which she is under obligation to carry her share of responsibility?

# THE CASE OF THE UNRULY CHILD

In metaphysical science, we do not preach but practice. Instead of condemning the seeming evil in a child, we call forth the good by recognition and realization. We make the good more attractive than the evil. If punishment is needed, we administer it without threat. Instead of teaching the child negative prayers to say before he goes to bed at night and when he arises in the morning—the times when the subconscious mind is most receptive to suggestion, we encourage him to repeat affirmations of truth that are constructive and life-giving. We never force or coerce him but encourage him to do those things which are for his highest good. When the parent becomes a partner instead of a dictator, punishment is seldom needed.

It is a rule in child-training that only repeated offenses demand attention. The objectionable act that becomes a habit has to be handled, but habits, good and bad, come, as we all know from experience, only by endless repetition.

The adult needs only to think of the many isolated mistakes he makes without being penalized to realize that his child has some rights in this direction.

The ideal kind of companionship between parents, and children lets a parent say something like this to a child in a temper, "I know you are angry and I know why. When I was your age, I would have been just as angry as you are I think. In fact, I still get angry at times when things go wrong. But you won't feel so bad about this in a little while, and you're not very pretty to look at now. Which would you rather do — go off by yourself for a while, or take a walk with me, or help bathe the dog?"

The    I-love-you-dearly-but-I-don't-like-what-you-are-doing attitude is easily sensed by the child. Assurance of love and of understanding gives a child a perspective on his conduct; fear makes him blind and irresponsible.

Amiel, the Swiss poet and philosopher, says in his *Journal Intime*, "The religion of a child depends on what its mother and father are, and not on what they say. The inner and unconscious ideal which guides their life is precisely what touches the child; their words, their remonstrances, their punishments, their bursts of feeling even, are for him merely thunder and comedy; what they worship, this it is which his instinct divines and reflects . . . . This is why the first principle of education is: train yourself; and the first rule to follow if you wish to possess yourself of a child's will is: master your own."

Parents must put first things first. Social and other activities cannot be placed ahead of the spiritual welfare of the child. Religion is not a milk chute put into the side of the house after it is built, but a spiritual atmosphere or foundation, pervading and supporting the whole structure. There is no substitute for religion.

# THE CASE OF THE ADOLESCENT

Nature sweeps children irresistibly into maturity. If they have had the right nurture, instruction, and training in the formative years of their existence, they will come through the difficult stage of adolescence and be normal, reliable, and sensible adults. The same power that brings them through the awkward period will take them beyond it.

The thoughtful parent will find much information and comfort in recent publications in the field of child growth and development. Characteristics of succeeding age-levels have been carefully charted. Often a newly-apparent characteristic that is extremely troublesome to a parent will be discovered to be a normal development. With this knowledge, the father and mother are in a position to supply guidance rather than suppression or punishment.

Parents should not try to coerce young people in making important decisions. Facts in the case as the adult sees them should be presented, but the decision should be their own. Only by this technique can be the growing youth move into acceptance of responsibility.

The important thing when teenagers get out of hand is to maintain calmness and composure. Harsh and ugly words, force, argument, and excitement play a part in the situation that has no bearing on it. The influence of parents is always strengthened by their composure. Altercations put a great strain on family relationships; they tend to develop fear or, worse still, a sense of pleasure in the excitement. It is difficult to realize how gratifying being the center of attention is and to what an extent the desire to receive attention is responsible for our actions.

The Chinese say that "In a broken nest, there are no whole eggs." When the home is broken, family unity and security are gone. To be inwardly homeless is to be confused. If you do not believe this, check the homes of the inmates of our reformatories. Preserve family unity, and everything else has a chance of coming out right. No matter what comes up to disrupt family relations, no matter how many altercations seem inevitable, the family must be kept together.

When there is discord and friction in the home, discuss the problem objectively. Put yourself in the other person's place and try to see the problem from his standpoint. Be as frank to confess your own sins as you are his, and peace and understanding will quickly return. Admitting your own faults is a sign of strength and not weakness. *"Let this mind be in you which was also in Christ Jesus."* Go into the Silence together and let God melt you into a common purpose and greater consciousness of Truth.

# SUGGESTED MEDITATIONS
# FOR THE HOME

THIS HOUSEHOLD IS A STRONG DEFENSE
AGAINST ALL EVIL, FOR IT IS THE ABODE
OF GOOD, OF LIFE, TRUTH, LOVE, WISDOM,
UNDERSTANDING, JOY, BEAUTY, ORDER,
POWER, AD PEACE.

THE MEMBERS OF THIS HOUSEHOLD ACCEPT
THEIR UNITY WITH THE ONE MIND – THE
*"MIND WHICH WAS ALSO IN CHRIST JESUS"*.
WE ACCEPT OUR RESPONSIBILITY AS
CHANNELS FOR THE TRUTH THAT WE KNOW
AS THE EXPRESSION OF UNIVERSAL LOVE
AND POWER. WE ARE GRATEFUL FOR OUR
AWARENESS OF THESE TRUTHS.

# FOR THE MOTHER

I AM A CENTER OF DIVINE LOVE. I RADIATE
LOVE TO EVERY MEMBER OF MY FAMILY.
THOSE WHO COME INTO MY HOME FEEL
THE POWER OF THIS ABIDING LOVE AND
COMRADESHIP AND ARE BLESSED BY IT. I
AM NOT DISTURBED BY ALTERCATIONS,
DISCORD, MISUNDERSTANDINGS, OR
RANCOR BECAUSE I KNOW THAT THE CHRIST
WITHIN ME IS GREATER THAN ALL THESE
THINGS. GOD'S LOVE OPERATING THROUGH
ME ATTRACTS NOTHING BUT GOOD TO ALL
IN THIS HOME. DEAR HEAVENLY FATHER,
I PLACE MY HUSBAND AND MY CHILDREN

LOVINGLY IN YOUR CARE. YOU ARE STRONG, WISE, AND EVER-PRESENT. I TRUST YOU TO BLESS, GUIDE, NOURISH, AND PROTECT THEM. HELP ME TO BE A GOOD WIFE AND MOTHER. HELP ME TO PUT MY KNOWLEDGE AND UNDERSTANDING OF MY UNITY WITH THEE INTO PRACTICE. HELP ME TO FEEL YOUR PRESENCE IN EVERY THOUGHT, WORD, AND ACTION SO THAT I MAY EXEMPLIFY FOR MY FAMILY ALL THAT IS RIGHT, AND TRUE, AND LOVELY. MAKE ME WORTHY OF THE RESPECT AND LOVE THAT MY CHILDREN GIVE ME.

# Raisa - Mystic Alchemist

## Energy Healing, Chakra Alignment, Sacred Geometry, Sound Healing

Tammy:
I was blessed with a healing session by Raisa last week. She felt like a friend and like-minded gentle soul with comforting Mother Mary essence pouring through her words. Raisa was so in-tuned to my blocks and traumas held within my field. She used her connection to ascended masters I've resonated with such as Yeshua, Mother Mary, Mary Magdalene, Lady Vesta & Amethyst and archangels Metatron, Michael and others to help clear these.

I was able to address childhood trauma situations to flip the stuck energy I've held onto over the years. She also picked up on a few traumatic past-life scenes that have affected my current life. I am an intuitive energy healer who truly felt the shift and healing within. I now feel so much lighter and have clarity regarding my path.

So much love and gratitude to you both, Raisa and Barry for presenting her to my world! (More Testimonials on following Pages)

Contact Raisa to book an Energy Healing
or Chakra Alignment session:
www.RaisinYourIsness.com
raisinyourisness@hotmail.com

Shannon:

This BEAUTIFUL sister...our Raisa... is a treasure beyond compare! After my experience in my personal session with Raisa... the ABSOLUTE confirmation I received, that could ONLY be confirmed by HER mind you... this session solidified EVERYTHING for me. I KNOW that this sister... she is a formidable, magnificent & IRREPLACEABLE component in this Earth plane story we all are invested in! IF YOU ARE DRAWN TO HER FOLLOW YOUR HEART

No other can do what SHE is gifted to do for YOU... YES YOU!

I LOVE YOU dear sister! I am forever grateful for what only you could do and DID for me! I would have happily paid any price for what you gave me! I URGE YOU ALL to schedule a session with this beloved one!

P.S. thank you Barry for sharing her with us all!

Natasha:

I would like to thank Barry for introducing us to Raisa. I have had 2 consultations with her in the last month and I am in total awe of what transpired. Raisa is such a beautiful caring soul! She connected with me as though she has known me forever. Her love and dedication in assisting others is so touching. I had an amazing experience and some profound healing. I received a message from Jeshua which brought tears to my eyes. I could feel the LOVE in the message that was given to me and I will remember and cherish His message forever. Raisa has really helped me in confronting fears, trauma and past life karma. I have found the reason for my skin problems which I never would have thought it'd be possible. It is amazing what guilt and shame from past lives can actually do to your body. Her healing and that from our Angelic beings has really made a huge difference in my life. I can feel it in my energy. Raisa has a lovely sense of humour, always reminding you not to take life and yourself so seriously. I really feel like a heavy weight has been lifted off my soul. Thank you so much! Much Love!

Ariel:

Raisa... Divine Raisa... You are a Treasure to this Life, and I thank All That Is, and this also Treasured YT channel for the priceless blessing which was our session this AM. Every moment of the session was a fractal explosion of wonderful intuitive & divinely guided perfection. I honor your sincere, caring, graceful, playful, soothing, encouraging, transformational, empowering, and so beautiful demonstration / embodiment of Goddess energy and presence. I am so honored & thankful to have been guided to You. To have invested in the patience, time, energy, and resources to share sacred healing and uplifting time with You. I will remember the session Always. And I will look forward to any and all ways our Creator deems it harmonious to connect again. I could go on and on and on, so please accept my parting acknowledgment of your blessing to this realm, my Heart & Spirt, my Life, and the Lives of all those who may be positively impacted via your assistance. Blessings, and Gratitude, a thousand times over and over again. Namaste... Namaste... Namaste...

B.G.

I have just finished a healing session with Raisa. The experience was remarkable! I am still buzzing! I heard about her from this channel, so thank you deeply Barry!

Raisa is so lovely to talk to, and intuitively guided, knows how to get to the hidden roots of our issues. She calls upon ascended masters, archangels and such to do deep energetic clearing and healing work. It was like being guided through the deep layers of myself, releasing the things that don't serve me and filling every cell with light. I purged, and I absorbed new energy, and came out feeling uplifted and renewed. Raisa helped me to find things in myself that I had been cut off from, and to heal wounds I had tried to bury. She has also given me helpful ideas to continue to improve things my life.

I am so blessed to have found Raisa, and ever grateful for the healing work she has done. She is as authentic as they come. Truly an earth angel! Thank you, thank you, thank you!

YouTube Channels of Interest:

## Giving Voice to the Wisdom of the Ages

Over 5,000 audios, hundreds of
Spiritual and Metaphysical
audio books including
Robert A Russell, Dr Murdo MacDonald Bayne,
Napoleon Hill, Jeshua, Kryon and many more.

## I AM Meditations and Affirmations

Hundreds of I AM Meditations,
Daily affirmations and more.

## Raisin' Your Isness

Metaphysical Musings, Channelings,
Sound Healing Songs